WHAT OTHERS ARE SAYING ABOUT THIS BOOK:

"Civil litigation exposure and insurance costs will drop dramatically with the adoption of the methods and techniques Newland has developed. In a lodging world replete with ever increasing costs, his innovations provide a unique and virtually cost-free approach. Every hotel management student should be required to read this textbook--I wish it had been available during my University and Lodging careers. --- **David C. Sullivan, Esq., Former VP and General Counsel, Motel 6 and University Counsel, University of Pittsburgh.**

"This approach to guest protection will be the industry standard and should be required reading for every lodging and security professional." --- **Robert F. Fitzgerald, Former Chief Operating Officer, Best Western International, Inc., and President, Worldwide Hospitality, Inc.**

"In this book, a new dimension is explored. The concept of protection is carefully examined. Coupled with that is the challenge to more effectively address the need for Reasonable Care....(my) compliments to the author." --- **Raymond C. Ellis, Jr., CHE, CHTP, Professor, Conrad N. Hilton College of Hotel and Restaurant Management, University of Houston.**

"No one in America is more qualified to write this book. Not just for hotel professionals, but for everyone concerned with premises liability--an absolute must." --- **Ernest J. Criscuoli, Jr., CPP, Former Executive Vice President, American Society for Industrial Security.**

"After a career in law enforcement, I enjoyed a second career in the lodging industry. In both cases, my prime responsibility was that of "protection." I have read and studied virtually every reference written on the subject and I can say without qualification that this is unquestionably the finest Lodging Guest Protection text ever written. --- **Richard C. "Rick" Clement, VP, TROP World Casino and Entertainment Resort, Atlantic City and Past President, International Association of Chiefs of Police (IACP.)**

HOTEL PROTECTION MANAGEMENT

THE INNKEEPER'S GUIDE TO GUEST PROTECTION AND REASONABLE CARE

LOREN E. NEWLAND, CPP, CHA

TNZ PUBLISHERS, INC.
SPOKANE, WASHINGTON

AMERICAN SOCIETY FOR INDUSTRIAL SECURITY
1625 PRINCE STREET
ALEXANDRIA, VA 22314
(703) 519-6200

HOTEL PROTECTION MANAGEMENT

THE INNKEEPER'S GUIDE TO GUEST PROTECTION AND REASONABLE CARE

Loren E. Newland, CPP, CHA

Published by:
TNZ PUBLISHERS, INC.
P. O. BOX 141647
SPOKANE, WA 99214
(509) 928 9514
fax (509) 922 6537

Library of Congress Cataloging-in-Publication Data
Loren E. Newland, CPP, CHA
Hotel Protection Management, The Innkeeper's
Guide to Guest Protection and Reasonable Care
96-61934

ISBN 1-886081-00-X

TABLE OF CONTENTS

PAGE

TABLE OF CONTENTS continued

PAGE

ACKNOWLEDGMENT

Scores of people have played a role in the development of this text - indeed the development of the theory and practice of Hotel Protection Management.

Betty Zachow, Senior Editor and Publisher, contributed untold hours of toil, concern and support as the text was begun, interrupted time and again, and begun time and again. It would not be in print today without her. Further, the unselfish technical support provided by Keith Zachow has been invaluable.

Robert Stein (Colonel, USAF, retired) filled the role (as no other I know could have) of initial reader/editor. As a published author, university professor, command pilot, manager and practitioner of safety and security, his broad prospective was unique. I am forever indebted to him.

Thanks to Ronald J. Oberholtzer, CPP; David Gyongyos, Esq., and Hayden Williams, who were major players during the initial development "in the field" of the Hotel Protection Management approach. They were with me at various times along the lecture tour as these approaches were initially introduced and refined. They will find many of their own words and thoughts throughout the text. Additionally, Oberholtzer unselfishly provided technical guidance and material in support of the chapter on Protection Officers.

A special thanks to Chris E. McGoey, CPP, whose works are referenced liberally throughout the text with his kind permission. It was he originally who urged the publication of this work.

Jack Galloway of Houston, TX provided invaluable insight into the rewriting and final editing process. He applied to this manuscript the same editorial sharpening which had earlier made him a successful journalist and author.

And a most special thanks to Professor Raymond C. Ellis, Jr., CHE, CHTP, of the Conrad N. Hilton College of Hotel and Restaurant Management, University of Houston. Professor Ellis undoubtedly knows more about guest protection and reasonable care than any other hotelier currently practicing. He, along with his hotel management students (particularly Mike Dossat, Amy Greene nee Aronowitz, and Tiffany Henderson) provided unique insight. They accepted the text, then incomplete and in disarray, and tested it in the best of settings - the classroom. Their comments were of enormous value.

The entire staff of the American Society for Industrial Security has been unfailingly supportive. Particular thanks are due to Eva Giercuszkiewcz and her associates in the Information Resource Center; technical protection and security information was provided virtually instantaneously over the several years this text was being researched. I owe that staff a great debt.

Technical printing support was provided by the ownership and staff of Alphagraphics of Scottsdale, AZ. They constantly went beyond the expected call of duty.

Finally, eternal gratitude to my family who suffered through boring and trying years of hearing about "the book." Their love and support immeasurably eased the load.

A WARNING ABOUT CRIME

Society has not been able to *prevent* crime.

Likewise, this textbook does not purport to be able to *prevent* crime.

Rather, this book is designed to provide students and practitioners of hotel management, methods of *deterring* crime and criminal acts.

It has been developed as a guide by which protection against crime can be integrated into an overall hotel management scheme. It presents methods, models and techniques which, when properly conceived, carefully installed and effectively maintained can aid in providing guest protection and reasonable care.

This text is neither designed nor should it be regarded as a guide to legal matters. On the contrary, readers should seek advice from legal experts whenever an issue of legality arises.

The purpose, simply, of this text is to educate.

Gender Usage Information

Few if any industries throughout our country have offered and continue to offer the opportunities for women that are offered in the hotel, motel and hospitality industries. Many of the highest positions currently are held by women who perform their work proudly and with excellence.

The use of the pronouns "he"and "him" in this book are used solely for the sake of simplicity and in no manner refer only to men.

DEDICATION

To my dear Mary Ann who makes it all happen and who makes it all worthwhile.

FOREWORD

Raymond C. Ellis, Jr. CHE, CHTP
Professor, Conrad N. Hilton College
University of Houston, Houston, Texas
1997

The closing decades of the twentieth century have brought a number of critical issues into focus for the lodging industry. It is interesting to note that the 1960s brought a concern for personal safety and accident prevention at the national level. Consequently, the hotel industry, along with the rest of the Nation, changes the way it dealt with the employee and the work safety of that employee as the Williams-Steiger Occupational Safety and Health Act of 1970 (OSHA) was enacted.

During the 1970s we looked to conservation and management of energy. The 1980s brought a focus that was peculiar to the lodging industry as arson fires and heavy loss of lives within hotel fires occurred. The 1990s have brought a similar situation in that there has been an unusual emphasis upon crime in the lodging establishment, fostered to a great extent by the media, even though the community crime situation was even more serious than that encountered within a lodging establishment.

The traditional methods addressing the "security" problem within the hotel or motel have been under scrutiny and there have been numerous techniques proposed to resolve the problem. Security hardware and security staff have been suggested. The argument has been made for involvement of the public, including the guest, the employee and the police. With this three-pronged approach, it was hoped there would be a resolution of the incidence of crime on the lodging premises. While some benefits have derived from this approach, it has not brought the desired final results.

In this book, a new dimension is explored. The concept of PROTECTION is carefully examined. Coupled with that is the challenge to more effectively address the need for REASONABLE

CARE. For too long there has been lip service within the industry to both of these concepts. The following pages will set an agenda for addressing these critical needs with the introduction of RESPONSIBILITY and ACCOUNTABILITY within each and every department of the lodging establishment.

You are urged to read these pages with an open mind; moving away from traditional approaches and the attitude noted by the author: "MANY PRACTICING INNKEEPERS WILL MENTALLY SCOFF AND SELF-RIGHTEOUSLY THINK: "ON MY PROPERTY, EVERYONE IS RESPONSIBLE FOR GUEST PROTECTION!!!" But the author asks, "Who is accountable for reasonable care and guest protection?" And I would add the question, "Is it the room attendant or the bellperson?" "Is it the kitchen worker or the second cook?"

In an interesting departure from the concept of BUILDING A BIGGER AND BETTER SECURITY DEPARTMENT AND STAFF, the author urges an emphasis on guest protection and reasonable care as a management tool employed by all senior, middle and supervisory management. This level of staff then becomes responsible if there is a breakdown in the provisions of reasonable care or adequate protection for the guest. On a department by department basis, there is no accountability for any such breakdown.

In this volume, you will be invited to adopt new approaches to challenges whose solutions have become more difficult and more elusive over the years. Obviously a management techniques that incorporates responsibility and accountability for guest protection and implementation of the doctrine of reasonable care can only be a MAJOR PLUS.

Welcome to a volume that will make the difference in how you provide reasonable care for, and the protection of the guest, and one might add, the general public and the employees, too. Often in the hospitality industry one sends "compliments to the chef, "So, here, I do send "compliments to the author."

EXECUTIVE SUMMARY OF PART ONE

HOTEL PROTECTION MANAGEMENT

Part One of Hotel Protection Management will lay the groundwork for the overriding theme of this text--that guest protection is an absolute requirement within the lodging industry.

The fact that guest protection should be such a paramount concern, on the face of it, seems simple, straightforward and non-controversial. To the uninitiated, such a statement seems almost innocuous----quite simply, a *given.*

Unfortunately, it is not.

On the contrary, the multitude of civil law cases in the court system suggest that such a statement is neither a given nor has it even been broadly accepted by the majority of our industry. We will discover that over the past two decades (since the infamous Connie Francis case in 1974) a litigious society, acting through a civil court system, has threatened and sometimes defeated segments of our industry.

These civil court actions have, following a death, injury or assault on a guest, attempted to prove that the lodging property involved was negligent in its duty to care for that guest--that the defendant property had, in other words, failed to provide Reasonable Care. All too often, the defendant property (and our industry) has been defeated in such litigations.

How is it possible, after over 20 years of experience (usually an unpleasant and costly experience) that we as an industry group continue to increasingly find ourselves held liable for failing to protect our number one asset, our guests?   As a modern, sophisticated industry, why have we apparently failed in this seemingly basic tenet?

Many hoteliers argue, with a considerable amount of evidence to support them, that we have made great strides in this area. In truth, many have. Chain after chain and property after property *have* developed programs aimed exclusively at such care and yet the litigation continues to rise. Why?

While the answers are neither clear-cut nor simple, we will examine possible root causes and explanations. Furthermore, we will look at the historic beginnings of Guest Care in the marketplace and in the court system, and we will investigate a possible answer to our industry's pervasive problem of providing the expected level of care.

We will learn about Hotel Protection Management.

CHAPTER ONE

CONNIE FRANCIS ...
THE TERRIBLE BEGINNING.

This is a text concerning management within the lodging industry. It is, however, probably unlike any lodging text previously published.

Its focus is that of Guest Protection and Reasonable Care, subjects which both strongly affect and threaten literally every employee in every department of every property of every lodging chain throughout the Nation.

The text addresses the most significant threat to each of those properties and each those chains--that of civil (sometimes criminal!) litigation which is brought against the property and which alleges failure to provide **Reasonable Care.**

It does more, however, than simply focus on the problem. It also offers solutions! These solutions, if objectively considered, adjusted to local conditions and applied, will reduce significantly (and cost-effectively) the threat of severe loss through civil litigation.

It is designed admittedly as a "How-To" text.

How to (as a traditional text) engrain in the college or university student, from his early-on exposure to this exciting industry group, knowledge of one absolute requirement. _That requirement is that the guest is the Innkeeper's first consideration, and protection for that guest must be the paramount concern throughout his career._

How to (as a practical on-property reference) provide to the lodging professional management-science techniques, methods and procedures which allow a systems approach to guest protection and reasonable care. This approach, when properly applied, not only protects the guest but significantly reduces costs, increases staff morale and facilitates enhanced property-wide departmental management.

How to (as a theoretical work) change the face of "security"--a counterproductive word. In the minds of most hoteliers, "security" conjures visions of a cigar-smoking, perhaps over-weight, retired police officer whose career has been one of *reacting* to a call. It is designed to change that image to one of a *proactive*, property-wide management program which can provide virtual certainty of Reasonable Care.

In short, this text will show how to protect the single asset needed to ensure our industry's survival: THE GUEST!

The text may cause reaction from lodging-industry readers ranging from distress to delight. Distress will come from some because of the suggestions that the industry often has failed to fulfill its management (as well as legal and moral) obligations to protect the guest; delight from others who will recognize the truth of the industry's dilemma and applaud an attempt to provide a unique and innovative solution.

This is not a legal text and must not be considered as such. The reader should turn to legal sources and legal authorities to learn the law. Rather, this is a text which is in *response* to the' law--the law which holds that guests have a right to a certain level of protection, and that the lodging industry has an obligation to provide it.

This is also a text about lodging management. It is not, however, a lodging management text in the traditional sense of the phrase.

Traditionally, lodging management texts concern themselves with a single management concern, either departmentally (F&B, or Housekeeping) or functionally (Finance or Personnel.) This text however addresses the aspect of lodging management which touches and affects *all* departments and touches *every* employee and *every* hard asset.

Finally, and perhaps most important, this is a text about **Guest Protection.**   It has been written because guest protection and reasonable care have previously not been incorporated into a single management focus.

While these subjects have long been recognized, they have been nebulous intangibles. Lodging managers have had difficulty getting their hands around them.   Now they can.

Connie Francis ought never to have been raped.

But she was.

In 1974, that famous popular singer's music was at the top of the charts.

On November 7 of that year she checked into a Howard Johnson property in Westbury, Long Island, New York. She was shown to a room, and then retired for the evening.   During early morning hours of the following day she was awakened and assaulted by an unidentified male intruder who had gained access to her room through a sliding glass door--a door which later was shown to be insecure.

Ms. Francis brought civil suit against the corporation. In this suit, Ms. Francis contended that the assault and rape inflicted upon her were due to the failure of the property to provide adequate security. Stated another way, she contended that the property had, in fact, *allowed* the assault by having failed to provide Guest Protection and Reasonable Care.

The sequence of events is well documented in legal literature and the eventual verdict is widely known. The case citation is Garzilli v. Howard Johnson's Motor Lodges, Inc., U.S. District Court, E.D. New York No. 75 C 979, Sept. 20, 1976.

Ms. Francis prevailed in her law suit and was awarded $2.5 million. And although the amount of the award was substantial, the impact of this case has gone far beyond any monetary considerations. The ripple effects of what hospitality practitioners refer to as the "Connie Francis case" have changed the concepts, the operations, the planning and arguably, the future and continued success of the lodging industry.

Many lodging professionals and lodging chains have taken the Connie Francis case to heart. They have attempted to adjust their methods of operations in order to neutralize or deter similar incidents.

Others have made halfhearted and usually inadequate attempts to achieve this same goal. Still others--and this category of hoteliers sadly may be in the majority--have failed to address the root problem. Simply put they have failed to provide Reasonable Care and Guest Protection. They are indeed <u>as tragically in peril as are their guests</u>.

It is not being melodramatic to assert that ignoring this issue places this group of hoteliers, their properties, their corporation, and their professional futures at untenable risk.

It is a strange dilemma: There is the obvious need to address guest protection. The courts demand it. The guests expect it. And failing to provide it can be literally fatal. In spite of this, a significant number of Innkeepers fail to take the necessary action. Why?

There are several possible answers:

(1) The subject of guest protection has, apparently, to many Innkeepers, a connotation which is thought to be contrary to the

concept of being a "Host." This apprehension and misapplied thinking likely exists because the subject of guest protection is usually understood and translated within the lodging industry as meaning "security." That connotation is limiting and negative and erroneous.

The text will discuss this term and its weaknesses and present a case for a new term, "protection," found in later chapters.

Innkeepers normally strive to present an image of openness and relaxation, of comfort and enjoyment. They strive to present that image which Innkeepers desire most to portray: that of a Friendly Host.

How then, many of them wonder, could they possibly introduce and employ the cold, hard reality of "security" when by its very nature "security" appears to be contrary to that host-image portrayal. This is a common mind-set of many Innkeepers. Arguably, it is a dangerously erroneous mind-set. In truth, the perfect host not only portrays all of these host-like characteristics, he also provides <u>a safe, secure environment</u>.

(2)   There is a second and closely related possible reason that guest protection is not adopted and effectively integrated into an overall property management scheme. Once the Innkeeper has developed a mind-set which equates "guest protection" to "security," he often mentally "compartmentalizes" the subject of guest protection into, and as a part of, that <u>negatively perceived security function</u>.

In the mind of many Innkeepers, "guest protection" equals "security" which equals a "Security Department." Such thinking automatically means that guest protection is not only a part of the negatively perceived security function, but also the *exclusive responsibility* of that department. This, too, is dangerously wrong.

It is thought that such a compartmentalized "Security Department" (and, by extension, guest protection), should have the responsibility for "doing" security. This thinking further suggests that all the protection the guest requires should be provided through a uniformed Security Force. This "Rent-A-Cop" or "Hire-an-Ex-Cop" thinking is as short sighted and dangerous as not addressing the guest protection problem at all.

(3)   A third possible cause for the less-than-universal acceptance of guest protection as an absolutely essential function within the lodging industry is just simple short-sightedness.

It is a combination of, "Crime can't be stopped anyway so why spend too much time and effort on it?" and "That's why we have insurance!" Add to these the "It-can't-happen-to-me" syndrome, and the stage is set for inaction, for loss potential, and in worst-case situations for total property failure.

Any or all of these three possibilities may be the root cause for the all-too-common failing to provide guest protection and reasonable care.

Indeed, there is probably one more reason for this serious and possibly fatal failing. The reason guest protection and reasonable care have never been given the management attention they deserve is that they have never been reduced to a single, hands-on, usable and understandable lodging management formula and approach.

The subject of Guest Protection and Reasonable Care, unlike virtually every other property-level management function, has seldom if ever been recognized as a total, functional entity to be adopted and properly managed.

Of even greater concern is the fact that seldom if ever has it been addressed and taught academically as an individual discipline.

The most prestigious authority in hospitality education, the Council on Hotel Restaurant and Institutional Education (CHRIE) bears this out.

CHRIE describes itself in its directory as "... a non-profit organization founded in 1946 devoted to the fostering of international advancement of teaching, training, leading, research and practice in the field of hospitality/tourism management, and to encourage and facilitate the professional development of CHRIE members."

It is, in short, the recognized authority in lodging-management higher and formal education. In the introduction of its third edition of A GUIDE TO COLLEGE PROGRAMS IN HOSPITALITY AND TOURISM, the organizational chart on the following page is shown. The chart, used by permission of CHRIE, presents virtually every commonly accepted departmental entity within a large typical property.

Further, it is an easy and obvious jump from this sample organizational chart to the actual management structure within most large properties. The chart then, is a pictorial representation of factual conditions--how many properties look, how they operate organizationally, <u>and how they are managed</u>.

Obviously, as shown on the chart and as practiced on the property, the Sales Manager heads (and therefore is assumed to manage), the sales function. The Front Desk Manager heads and manages the front desk function. The Food and Beverage Manager heads and manages the F&B function.

But there is one obvious and unacceptable omission--in both the sample organizational chart (theory) and in the property management scheme (practice). <u>There is no indication of who manages Guest Protection and Reasonable Care</u>. That subject (as an entity within the organizational chart) is absent--ignored. That subject, as a management practice on the property, also is often ignored.

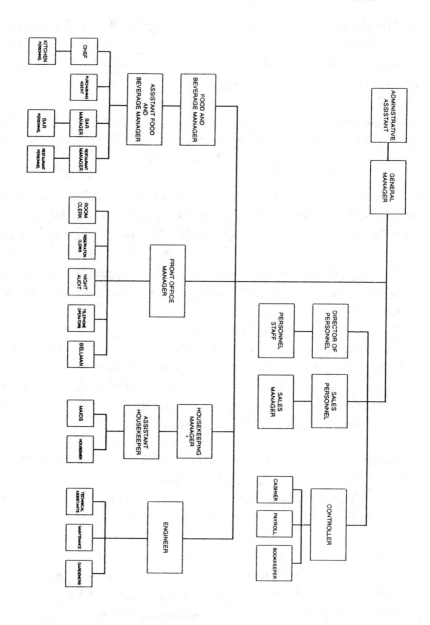

Used by permission of CHRIE, the original chart shown as Figure 9, page 17 of the third edition of
A GUIDE TO COLLEGE PROGRAMS IN HOSPITALITY AND TOURISM.

At this point in the reading of this text, many practicing Innkeepers, (and possibly students) will mentally scoff and self-righteously think: "On my property, everyone is responsible for guest protection!"

That reaction is the one which the author almost invariably receives while presenting seminars on Guest Protection.

"Everyone is responsible for guest protection and reasonable care is everyone's job." These are lovely thoughts--but *in the abstract and without protection management planning* they are as inaccurate as they are functionally improbable and short-sighted.

They are major and dangerous errors because they ignore one of the most basic tenets of management:

With responsibility comes accountability.

Ignoring this universally accepted management basic is at the core of the lodging industry's failure to properly address guest protection and reasonable care.

Example: If it is the case that the F&B manager is <u>responsible</u> for the F&B function (which he is) then too, he must be <u>accountable</u> for that function.

Another example: A guest, on a comment card, extols the Beef Wellington he was served in the property's restaurant. Subsequently, the GM receives and reviews this most favorable comment. If he is a forward-thinking GM, he could be expected to compliment the F&B Manager and somehow reward and reinforce this apparent manifestation of his superior management (and culinary) skills.

By this same contemporary management thinking, it also could be expected that the GM will somehow motivate and correct that same F&B Manager if and when a guest rightfully complains of poor service in the dining room. The GM expects, and rightfully so, exemplary performance. However, when the occasion arises, he correctly responds to negative performance. In effect, he holds the offending manager accountable.

There are indeed two sides to the one management coin, and these two sides are Responsibility and Accountability. It follows, then, that the <u>responsibility</u> for guest protection must be assigned, and the assignee must be held <u>accountable</u>. Without having assigned such responsibility and accountability, <u>no one</u> is responsible and <u>no one</u> can be held accountable.

When the rape occurs, when the assault happens, when the guest is burglarized, <u>unless someone has been assigned the responsibility, there will be no one to hold accountable</u>. The result is that all too often nothing is corrected.

Therefor in terms of guest protection and reasonable care, the lodging manager *must* assign responsibility and demand accountability.

The F&B Manager is responsible for the F&B function--he also must be accountable. The Sales Manager is responsible for the Sales function--he also must be accountable. The Front Desk Manager is responsible for the front desk functions--he also must be accountable. The Chief Engineer is responsible for the engineering function--he also must be accountable.

But who is responsible for and accountable for guest protection and reasonable care?

The answer to that question constitutes not only the content of, but the reason for this text book.

CHAPTER TWO

HOTEL PROTECTION MANAGEMENT

THEORY

In a perfect world, commercial and business success would be determined exclusively in the marketplace.

Hard work, good planning and effective management would virtually guarantee financial rewards. In the lodging industry, we would acquire the ideal hotel location, invest in building and development, establish and maintain a productive work force, serve our clientele well and reap the rewards.

Unfortunately, the world is not perfect.

Sadly, and often disastrously, in the lodging industry, the exclusive and paramount importance of the marketplace has been replaced by the awesome and seemingly uncontrollable threat of the courtroom.

A property owner/manager can be blessed with the most ideal of locations, acquire and manage a superlative staff, provide the utmost in accommodations and services, and yet be doomed to financial and professional failure. With increasing frequency, hoteliers are victims of civil complaints (usually from guests) which lead to long, exhausting, untenable and expensive civil court proceedings. Often such litigation alleges the property owner/manager to be negligent in providing reasonable care.

More frightening still is the fact that a high percentage of such suits result in verdicts and judgements for the plaintiff--the guest who alleged inadequate care. Properties are ruined. Careers are over. In short, the importance of the marketplace has been undermined by the power of the civil court.

To demonstrate how pervasive the litigious thinking is throughout our society, ask a fellow-lodging student or practitioner to tell you the first thing which comes to his mind when you mention the "MGM Grand."   What comes to mind, of course, is the terrible fire which that Las Vegas property experienced in the early 1980s. The ensuing lawsuits and years of litigation and eventual judgments consumed millions and millions of dollars.

The MGM Grand was, before this disaster, a magnificent property-- well placed, well managed, well staffed, and enjoying profitability and high occupancy. Today, as the MGM Grand, that property does not exist.

Throughout our industry, horror stories abound reflecting civil court decisions which have brought properties and managers to their knees and to oblivion.   These were decisions which, justly or unjustly, depending on your viewpoint, have been based on the charge that the property failed in its obligation to protect its guests.

It is a cruel and difficult fact of lodging life, but a fact nevertheless, that as we manage not only our departments, our properties, our regions, and our chains . . .

WE MUST ALSO MANAGE PROTECTION.

Just as we have had to learn to *drive* defensively on our streets, we must also learn to *manage* defensively in our professional lives. We must learn to integrate guest protection techniques and practices into our normal management approaches.

The days of a carefree Sunday drive when one could enjoy the pleasures of the drive and not worry about the surrounding dangers, are gone.

Also gone are the days of lodging management when the lodging manager could concern himself only with those satisfying functional aspects of our industry.

A highly effective F&B operation, even one offering superb cuisine, simply is not acceptable without guest protection.

A well-managed Rooms Department, without an eye toward reasonable care, should and must be a thing of the past.

The guest has come to expect protection; the courts have decreed that we must provide protection; we cannot survive unless we do provide protection.

A major question, however, even among those forward-thinking hoteliers who recognize the requirement to provide guest protection, has not been *whether* to provide such care but *how* to provide it.

We strive to be the perfect host. By word, act, appearance, and design we attempt to send the message to our patrons that they are, indeed, like guests in our homes. But how, for example, can we portray that image in the midst of a covey of armed guards?

We strive to provide easy and friendly access to our properties. How can we succeed at that and at the same time limit or deny access to those we wish to exclude?

We design our rooms to be comfortable, inviting and attractive. Isn't it a seeming contradiction to transpose such a welcoming room into one which is bedecked with locks, safety devices and protection equipment?

How can it be possible to remain effectively on both sides of the fence? How can we, on one hand, present the friendly, open and inviting atmosphere which the perfect host portrays and at the same time in a seemingly opposite mode, establish and maintain a "protection profile" which adequately provides reasonable care to our guests?

The answer lies in the implementation of *Theory and Practice of Hotel Protection Management.*

Hotel protection management consists of an integrated management model and series of approaches which, when properly applied, allow for the establishment and maintenance of an acceptable level of protection. And at the same time the image of hospitality is maintained. Four steps are involved in the development of the hotel protection model.

    (1)   Identifying and evaluating assets which must be protected

    (2)   Identifying and evaluating the threats which exist to those assets

    (3)   Employing a series of countermeasures designed to minimize those threats

    (4)   Developing a protection profile system from the above listed property-unique aspects and applying accepted management-science techniques thereto

This methodology has not been developed in the abstract. On the contrary, it has evolved from the totality of the three titular terms: (1) hotel, (2) protection, and (3) management.

HOTEL

Today's typical travelers are worlds apart from their counterparts a century or even a few decades ago. Not only do they have virtually an unlimited choice of means of travel, they have an exceptionally broad choice of accommodations when they reach their destination.

Consider some of the choices a traveler has when he reaches his destination.

*   A luxury full-service hotel
*   A modest hotel offering limited service
*   A roadside motel
*   A bed-and-breakfast establishment
*   A timesharing establishment
*   A resort
*   An apartment hotel
*   A campsite

And the list goes on and on--from modest to luxurious, from full-service to virtually do-it-yourself. From casino resorts to private clubs, the traveler has never had such a selection from which to choose.

Further, the traveler can avail himself of a property which functions as a multi-operation facility, at the same time offering long-term accommodations to some (an apartment), both room and food to others (a boarding house), and finally supplying the basic needs of an overnight guest (a traditional hotel.)

What is important to the student of lodging management is that for all practical purposes, there is little legal difference between any of these types of facilities when it comes to hotel protection management.

The legal definition of inns and hotels can be traced to several legal decisions dating from the late 16th century.

These early legal definitions vary to such a degree that it is difficult for a lay person to derive a common definition. However, in Juengel

v. City of Glendale (Mo. 1942) non-legally trained hoteliers can get more definitive and useful legal definition. It reads in part:

> "... a hotel is defined as a house which is held out to the public as a place where all transient persons who come will be received and entertained as guests for business, with food and lodging while on their journey; or a house where travelers are furnished with everything which they have occasion for while upon their way; or a place where transient guests are admitted to lodge, as well as one where they are fed and lodged ..."

And so, for the most part, these general descriptions seem to fit our common perception of hotels and inns. Further, the terms "Innkeeper," "Hotelkeeper," and "Hotelier" are used interchangeably.

Likewise, the term "motel," for all practical purposes, may be used as synonymous with "hotel" and "inn." For the purposes of this text, we should consider all these various forms of accommodations as "hotel"--the term we will use throughout.

This, then, is our "hotel", the first word in our title Hotel Protection Management.

It is to one of these establishments the guest goes with the expectation of service. An integral part of that "service" he expects to receive is the second term in our three-term title--protection.

PROTECTION

In chapter one, several possible reasons were advanced explaining why the concept of guest protection and reasonable care has not been universally accepted and adopted, even though it is recognized as a necessity within our industry.

Probably adding to all of those possible reasons is the fact that lodging managers have been besieged with a multiplicity of terms which seem to surround the subject of guest protection. These terms, in and of themselves, seem ill-defined, perhaps non-defined, and certainly confusing.

The following terms are bandied around constantly. They may be separate and distinct to the professional who deals with protection on a full time basis, to the average lodging manager, they may be confusing. They include the following:

*   Security
*   Risk control
*   Safety
*   Life-safety
*   Loss prevention
*   Asset protection
*   Loss control
*   Loss reduction
*   Crime prevention

And while the list goes on and on, there is an easy and helpful solution to the confusion. The industry is well advised to adopt a single, descriptive and extremely useful term to replace _all_ the ill-defined terms used above.

That word is **protection.**

Protection is defined as the state of being protected--the covering or shielding from harm, injury or destruction.

An examination of this definition will cause some inferences which might not be readily apparent. "Shielding from harm" seems to imply that the acts of protecting must, by definition, be proactive. If one is "shielded" from harm, then it seems evident that the harm will not be allowed to reach the person being protected.

Such a definition suggests that a barrier, or protective shield, or line of defense has been established which decreases the possibility and probability of the danger ever reaching and harming or causing loss to the one being protected.

Such action does not, it would seem, prevent the loss by attacking the potential "doer" of the harm. Rather, by surrounding the intended victim of the harm, it has the effect of reducing the possibility of the harm being inflicted.

It does not, in the case of the threat of *crime*, claim to "prevent." Rather it aims to deter the criminal act from ever reaching the target victim. Again, by definition, by design, and by necessity, protection is proactive. As such "shield" or barrier or protective techniques which acts as the deterrent must be in place *prior* to the threat ever occurring.

"Protection" is not "enforcement." Again, as we are using the term here as the second word in Hotel Protection Management, it is proactive rather than reactive. As such, it differs from the traditional role of the police.

To illustrate, the following is a random list of duties for which police are traditionally responsible:

* Respond to emergency calls
* Provide emergency assistance
* Investigate criminal acts
* Apprehend and interrogate suspects
* Question victims and witnesses
* Arrest and incarcerate suspected criminals
* Process suspected criminals into and through the appropriate criminal justice system in preparation for their appearance before the courts.

Each of these tasks is necessary, justified, expected, even demanded by society, yet each and every one of these tasks is *reactive.* They occur after the event has taken place.

While municipal police vehicles commonly advertise "Protect and Serve," it seems clear that the "protection" which is afforded is not the proactive "before-the-event-occurs" approach we must develop within our properties.

A review of the list of duties shows that police devote an extraordinary amount of time to an event (read that as crime) *after* it occurs. *We in the private sector (the lodging industry) must do just the opposite.* We must provide protection, not simply what is considered "security," before the event occurs.

The use of the term "security" can be a problem in and of itself, and its usefulness as the term to define "protection" may have run its course. It can be argued that the term causes a mis-focus and should not be used in a modern proactive, management-science-based property protection program.

There are several reasons for this assertion, not the least of which is the fact that the term "security" conjures visions of a "security officer," "Private Police" and/or a "Security Department."

Such envisioning has a dual disadvantage. It suggests that the responsibility of guest protection is limited to those "security" individuals and "security" departments, and worse yet, that such care is their exclusive responsibility.

This perception is both invalid and dangerous. Admittedly, the term "security" has been used throughout the text. Such use, however, is for the purpose of explanation and because the term is of such common and wide usage. "Protection" (rather than "security") then is the second term of our phrase Hotel Protection Management. It can perhaps best be defined as *efforts and techniques, methods and equipment, designed and in place, which deter the likelihood that harm or loss will occur.*

And we are left with our third and final word:

MANAGEMENT

Management is defined as "The art or act of managing, directing, facilitating or ascertaining the successful accomplishment of tasks or the attainment of stated objectives."

As stated earlier, this text is to some extent, a work about management. However, just as it is a text concerning law and is not a legal text, so also is it a text about management but does not claim to be a management text.

The reader who desires or needs management training has a world of resources to which he may turn. There is probably, in contemporary "how-to" literature, no other subject about which more has been written.

Every manager, every educator, every author who thinks he has a new angle on management is quick to name it, quick to publish it and quick to market it. The reality, however, is probably akin to the old adage that there is little, if anything, new under the sun.

In its simplest form management can best be described as that discipline designed and used to get tasks accomplished.

This simple definition denigrate the fact that much of today's modern management theory is steeped in and has been developed from theories which were initially university-based.

From the early university psychologist/educators, the science of management has been strongly influenced by academia. From

McGregor's Theory X Theory Y to Behavioral Sciences and Quantitative Approaches, virtually all management approaches have their roots in the university setting. The lodging management student should not consider his undergraduate or graduate studies complete without a thorough investigation of various management theories and approaches.

Consider our little clown.

THE **M** TOOLS

He is our model manager and the tools he has at his disposal are the same tools every manager has to some degree. They are called the "M" tools and they are the tools he uses to accomplish tasks. The four "Ms" represent Money, Methods, Machinery and Manpower.

To one extent or another, these are the tools which every manager has as he strives to accomplishes his objectives. He learns to influence and motivate and make most productive his "Manpower" tools and leads. He learns to develop, adjust and maintain ways and means of getting tasks done reasonably by his tool labeled "Methods." He learns to understand and utilize mechanical and electrical technology which has been developed over the years and his "Machinery" tools come into play. Finally, he learns to make the best use of his fiscal resources and how to spend and invest and budget them most efficiently and his "Money" tools are used.

Each of the four "M" tools, individually utilized and manipulated in concert with the other three, provide the manager with the ability to become effective. And behind each of these tools and the particular management disciplines they represent are vast stores of research and reference material upon which to draw.

From universities to libraries and to modern informational storage and multimedia resources, the student and practitioner of "management" may reach out for guidance. He can find techniques and management models and approaches to assist in solving the problems at hand. Such techniques, models and approaches *relative to hotel protection management* are provided in the ensuing chapters.

POINTS TO PONDER

HOTEL PROTECTION MANAGEMENT THEORY

◆   Discuss the reasons that it is essential to provide reasonable care to the guest.

◆   Define "Hotel Protection Management."

◆   Name the four steps involved in the development of a hotel protection model.

◆   Define the term "Protection."

◆   Discuss how "protection", as used in this text, differs from "enforcement" as practiced by police agencies.

◆   Define the term "Management."

◆   Name the four "M" (management) tools described in the text.

CHAPTER THREE

THE LAWS AFFECTING THE LODGING INDUSTRY

The expression *The Law* is commonly used by people to justify, to explain, to accuse and to defend their own actions and the actions of others.

"You can't do that--it's against the law!"

"I'm within my rights, under the law!"

"He's breaking the law!"

These and many other similar expressions are uttered and heard often by persons throughout the civilized world.

It has been said that the United States is not a nation of individuals but a nation of laws. As such, it behooves us both as citizens and as hoteliers to know something about the law, how it protects and affects us, and how it certainly impacts us as lodging professionals.

As a departure point, it should be understood that all law (including law related to lodging) is dynamic, which is contrary to popular opinion that it is concrete and unchanging. Not only does the law move, but such movement is caused by and reflective of the evolution of the society it supports and attempts to influence.

It is one's individual decision, as a private citizen, how little or how much of the law with which to become familiar. As a *hotelier*, however, it is imperative that he becomes familiar with that portion of the law which so deeply and severely affects our industry.

Lodging law, like all law, is a living breathing entity which is constantly changing. To ignore it and those changes is to put oneself as a hotelier, in peril.

Generality, the laws by which the lodging industry is governed, came from old English common law--that system of legal thought which forms the basis for the laws which exist today in most states.

For purposes of this book, there is a single, overriding and paramount requirement which every person involved in the lodging profession must bear in mind: **Protection of the guest is an absolute requirement.**

While old basic common law has evolved greatly over the years by judicial precedent, and many exceptions apply, it cannot be overemphasized that **protection of the guest is an absolute requirement.**

That fact and how to attain appropriate protection for the guest is the theme of this text.

A primary and very basic explanation of the law is in order, as it affects us as Innkeepers. The majority of this text is limited to an emphasis on civil rather than criminal law.

This is not to say that Innkeepers are not governed or influenced by the criminal codes--on the contrary just as every citizen is held to those guidelines and restraints, so also are Innkeepers. However, in your day-to-day conduct of lodging business, the civil aspects of the law are the ones with which you most often will come into contact. And, to state again for emphasis, the most vital civil law lesson which must be learned and practiced by lodging professionals is that **protection of the guest is an absolute requirement.**

A BIT OF HISTORY

The roots of our entire legal system (certainly including the laws which influence Innkeepers) may be found in England. During the middle ages (from approximately A.D. 500 to 1500) travel was not uncommon in that country.

While significant commerce was difficult at best because of the conditions of the roads, travel by foot, horse and light wagon was at a surprisingly high level. In addition to the roads being in deplorable condition, they offered another obstacle--they were infested with robbers, thieves and any number of other miscreants.

Our common vision of Old England with numerous and thick forests is fairly accurate. It is true that these criminals used the woodlands as their bases and for their protection (shades of Robin Hood and Sherwood Forest!) As dangerous as travel was during daylight hours, darkness brought even more danger. The traveler knew well he had best secure himself for the night.

He was limited in the amount of provisions he could carry, and with the added limitation of daylight movement, the traveler had to seek added protection and comfort.

As in all matters of business, supply and demand prevailed. In answer to the needs and demands of the traveler, lodging establishments were developed and the hospitality industry as we know it today was begun.

These earliest establishments included religious houses which catered both to nobles and to the poor. Principally, however, private homes constituted the majority of these establishments. They were converted in total or in part as temporary accommodations catering to the traveler's need for food, lodging, entertainment and protection. And from these early homes came the English Inn.

The Inn, or public house, looked much like the private home from which it evolved. It centered, as did the private home, around the Great Room, where much of the life spent indoors was concentrated.

Other parts of the Inn were added as required, and private quarters were common for the owner and Innkeepers. The majority of the inhabitants including servants, workers and various classes of guests gathered, entertained themselves, ate and eventually slept in the Great Room. Light was provided by candle and heat by a fireplace. And after the meal and at bedtime, the tables were converted to beds and the Great Room became a Great Common Bedroom. All this evolved from the private English home along the travel roadway.

As the art (and the profit) of accommodations advanced, inns began appearing which were being planned and constructed as just that-- inns. More space was provided and in some cases somewhat more privacy was possible, for a price. Yet even with these advances, it must be assumed that the majority of travelers, along with their horses which were tended in adjoining stables, were expected to eat and eventually sleep surrounded by less than perfect conditions. They shared not only their sleeping quarters but many times their beds with strange fellow-travelers.

Thus, the conditions evolved. The land/home owner who opened his home to the traveler became an Innkeeper as a businessman operating in this public arena. As such, his obligation became, as a public businessman, to serve all the public--to provide food and lodging and *protection.*

Restrictions, variances and peculiarities notwithstanding, such obligations exist today. As Innkeepers we provide food and lodging and **we protect the guest within the context of reasonable care.**

REASONABLE CARE

The courts demand it. The guests expect it. And we must provide it.

But what is it? What is reasonable care?

How do we identify it? Isolate it? Develop it?

How do we apply it? Measure it? How can we be assured we are, as required, providing it?

Let's take one step at a time.

Reasonable care.   Simply stated, it is the Innkeeper's duty to take sufficient reasonable care of his guests that they do not become victims of loss (loss being defined as injury, accident, criminal act or fire trauma.)

For the most part, the Innkeeper is not an insurer of the guest's safety. However, he is responsible for reasonable care of that guest, and in the absence of such care he may be held liable.

This is, in lay language, what the courts have said. We, as Innkeepers, must provide reasonable care. If the failure to provide such care is proven and a guest suffers a loss, we can be held liable.

Many hoteliers complain, and with justification, that the courts demand reasonable care and yet *seemingly have not issued a broad, quantifiable and measurable definition of it.*

On one hand, the courts have required that we provide a specified level of care and warned that failure to provide that level can cause great financial liability. And yet on the other hand, the courts have not established easily definable benchmarks against which that attainment can be measured. As we examine this apparent quandary, we will discover why the contradiction exists and how we can and must solve it.

One broad definition is that reasonable care is that level of care which a reasonable person has a right to expect under normal circumstances. Obviously, such a definition leaves much to circumstance and to subjectivity. Such ambiguity has led to a tongue-in-cheek definition-- reasonable care is "what the jury decides it is." And perhaps this definition is more than just a flippant attempt to define the undefined. As we progress through this text, it is essential to keep in mind that if the jury decides we did indeed provide reasonable care, then in fact we did provide it. We must also keep in mind that if the jury decides we did not provide such care, then indeed we did not!

Is it not apparent that we as hoteliers must be prepared to show that jury that the former was true?

Is it not obvious that we should establish a system--a program--an approach--A GUEST PROTECTION PROGRAM which would convince any jury of our peers that such reasonable care was in effect? Consider the advantages of a scheme which:

*   Protects the guest
*   Increases staff morale
*   Progressively impacts <u>favorably</u> on occupancy
*   Convinces the court that we provide reasonable care.

This is what Hotel Protection Management aims to do!

The first step in developing such a scheme is clarifying some basic ground rules, keeping in mind our prime objective: to protect the guest in order to avoid liability.

There are those who will say that such a statement is cold-blooded, cynical and certainly not in the best interest of lodging. Why should avoidance of civil liability be the prime motivation for the establishing and maintaining of a program of reasonable care?

Should not the care of the guest himself, irrespective of any civil obligations, be the paramount concern? The answer is, obviously, yes. Such guest care should be first and foremost. What is often overlooked, however, is that by the act of establishing such guest protection programs (admittedly as a shield against civil liability) we are also insuring such guest and care.

As we begin this process, it is important to establish that there are certain elements within the law which must be proven before a judgement of liability against the Innkeeper can be imposed. If the Innkeeper is to be judged guilty of liability, following an incident involving a guest, it must be shown that:

(1)   The Innkeeper had a duty to provide care to the guest
(2)   The incident was *foreseeable*
(3)   The Innkeeper failed to provide reasonable care
(4)   Such failure to provide reasonable care caused the incident to the guest
(5)   The guest suffered a loss (death, injury, loss of property, etc.) as a further result of the Innkeeper's failure to provide such care.

The court and/or the jury will address and decide upon these elements. It is in our best interest to recognize and understand that of these five elements, the two which we as Innkeepers are most able to address are (2), the foreseeability issue, and (3) the question of reasonable care. It is valuable and in fact necessary to address foreseeability first.

FORESEEABILITY

As stated above, foreseeability must be considered when determining liability. And, unfortunately, just as in the case of reasonable care, the definition of foreseeability, historically, has been imprecise and almost entirely subjective.

Broadly speaking, foreseeability, from a hotelier's standpoint, is that set of circumstances surrounding conditions about which the lodging manager had knowledge beforehand or *of which he should have had knowledge.*

Stated another way, a judgment of liability requires a degree of foreseeability. It requires that the event which occurred must have been foreseeable in the mind of the Innkeeper. A no-liability judgment was rendered in the case of a random killing of patrons in a fast-food restaurant in San Diego because the act, in the judgment of the court, was so outrageous and so completely unpredictable as to be not foreseeable. Protection *against* the possibility of that act, then, was not a requirement of the owner. However, had similar crimes been in evidence--a history of drive-by shootings, for instance, the judgment might well have been otherwise.

To review, Innkeepers can be held liable and suffer penalties if they fail to provide reasonable care, and a necessary ingredient in that verdict of liability is the fact of foreseeability. Was the Innkeeper aware of risks involved, or by the same token, *should he have been aware of such risks?* Given these circumstances, it seems prudent for the knowledgeable and sophisticated Innkeeper to begin his guest protection program by determining the identity and severity of surrounding threats. He needs to know what is foreseeable.

At this point, it is appropriate to give credit and accolades to Chris E. McGoey, CPP (Certified Protection Professional) a nationally acclaimed security consultant, author and expert witness.

McGoey, who specializes in premises liability, has filled a previous void and developed a model and approach for qualifying foreseeability. His book, *"Security, Adequate . . . or not: The Complete Guide to Premises Liability Litigation"* is a benchmark work written in layman language.

How is foreseeability determined from the hotelier's standpoint? Three factors initially enter into consideration:

(1)   The nature of the premises
(2)   Crime demographics
(3)   Location

Each of these considerations is enumerated from the standpoint foreseeability of crime in any public access facility. In this text, we have transposed these considerations into our area of premises liability concern--that of the hotel.

McGoey postulates that when referring to expert testimony presented to a Court that "An established criterion for determining a level of crime foreseeability must be utilized in order to provide a sound basis for opinion testimony."

No less is true for the Innkeeper establishing and maintaining his guest protection program. He must have a criterion from which to build his protection profile.

That criteria will allow for a complete analysis, the results of which "...will identify a level of crime foreseeability, which can be used to evaluate the adequacy of an existing security program on a premises." Again, transposing position into the lodging industry, the same analysis will allow the Innkeeper to evaluate the type and amount and nature of the protection he needs to establish in order to provide reasonable care.

NATURE OF THE PREMISES

The nature of the premises in question impacts on the subject of foreseeability. If the premise in question is, for instance, a jewelry store, the foreseeability of armed robbers is more likely to be higher than the foreseeability of the crime of obscene phone calls, irrespective of the seriousness of the crimes being compared.

By the same logic, the type of establishment within the same grouping impacts on the foreseeability of the type crime in question. For instance, The likelihood that the crime of room theft in a hotel would occur is, obviously, higher than that of embezzlement.

It is equally true that a hotel which has a high-energy lounge, caters to a younger crowd and demands a higher percentage of return on liquor sales could expect more and different crime problems than a property catering to a retirement-aged clientele.

It seems obvious that not only the type of premises by the use thereof will have an influence on foreseeability. Considerations include hours of operation, types of products and services offered, classification of clientele, age and experience of staff as well as the size, age and design of the property itself. These are but some of the considerations to be examined and analyzed by the GM and the Protection Management Committee which will be discussed in later chapters.

CRIME DEMOGRAPHICS

McGoey talks about crime demographics as follows:

"Elements involved in evaluating previous crime are a determination of which crime classifications are relevant, the relevant radius around the incident, the proper time frame, the type and precision of data available, and an estimate of the proportion of crimes that are officially documented."

He correctly states that these considerations, when viewed collectively and in concert with one another provide a basis for foreseeability determination that is much more accurate and useful than simply raw numbers.

The tongue-in-cheek question is often asked, "Do all fisherman lie, or do all liars fish?" A similar dilemma exists in raw crime numbers, specifically those reported by the FBI in their annual reporting of crime statistics. This dilemma, when realized, causes a person interested in foreseeability as a function of crime to be cautious.

Many factors can skew data and distort reality. For instance:

Many crimes go unreported by the victims.

Crimes which occur to a victim on a public premise (e.g., a hotel) often go unreported by the *premises*.

"Official crime statistics" are grouped geographically into boundary segments (census tracts) which may or may not accurately reflect those statistics relative to the subject property. A property may be, according to the FBI statistics, a relatively low crime area, but the fact that the property is in reality at the very edge of the boundary and adjoins a statistically *high* crime rate area does not disclose itself in the raw data.

Crime "categories" are often not reflective of the crime itself. The author, for instance, once testified in defense of a property in which "a series of sexual crimes" had been reported and the plaintiff was attempting to use this "fact" as a basis for proving that the hotelier should have been aware of such a nefarious threat. Upon examination it turned out

49

that the "series" consisted of three instances over a long period of time and the"sex crimes" turned out to be a peeping Tom! Hardly the foreseeability factor which a serial rapist would represent and which, according to the statistics would also be represented by "a series of sexual crimes."

Finally, and perhaps as important as any other "crime stat" factor is the fact that it is not uncommon for reporting agencies (local police departments, for instance) to either under- or over-report crime for their own purposes. Low reporting might show police agency success or high reporting might indicate a means of justifying added staff.

It becomes patently obvious, therefore, that raw crime data used to the exclusion of other related data is greatly suspect and invites incorrect analysis. Rather, crime demographics represent a compilation of statistics that is more precise and informative and valid than simply raw numbers.

LOCATION

McGoey suggests that the location, as one foreseeability factor among the three under consideration, is the *least substantial.* Its relative importance is generally subject to what has been found through investigation of the other two factors. It is the most likely to be influenced by physical conditions such as fences, foliage, signs, etc., and procedural conditions such as locking schedules, security patrol methods and incident reporting systems.

There are several elements impacting on this factor:

> * General location in the city
> * Relationship to other businesses and residences
> * Population density
> * Economic demographics of the relevant area

*   Proximity to major traffic arterial
*   The floor level within a building, in a common area or semi-private area

McGoey concludes that, "The concept of location as a major factor causes us to focus on the 'where' issue in crime foreseeability." All crime types are not foreseeable everywhere.

A rapist who gained access through a fourth floor exterior window of a high-rise apartment by using superior mountain climbing skill would not be reasonably anticipated and therefore not normally foreseeable.

However, a recently constructed 24-hour convenience store in the center of the highest crime zone in the city should anticipate a variety of property and personal crimes because of its location alone. Its level of crime foreseeability should be considered as potentially moderate to high from opening day.

Its actual level and type of crime foreseeability will be modified later and affected by the actual nature of the business and its ability to control criminal activity through use of security techniques.

These three factors, then, constitute a basis for an evaluation of foreseeability. Of much greater importance to the Innkeeper, however, is the fact that they offer the same departure point from which to either evaluate foreseeability in the establishment of a guest protection program or when measuring the adequacy of an existing program.

Knowledge of the levels of foreseeability is a necessary ingredient in the hands of the Innkeeper when he determines or measures his hotel protection management defenses against the threats which such foreseeability discloses.

Analysis of the three factors discussed above--the nature of the premises, crime demographics, and location--allows an Innkeeper to evaluate the level of foreseeability and respond with protective measures which are appropriate. The levels of foreseeability consist of (1) non-foreseeability, (2) low, (3) moderate, or (4) high.

NON FORESEEABILITY

Non-foreseeability is an absolute. If analysis of the foreseeability factors (premises, crime demographics and location) discloses the absence of facts which could allow any other level of foreseeability, then the occurrence of that particular event is "not-foreseeable." Such a determination might be made by an Innkeeper, following the gathering of available data, by total absence of prior similar crime or a determination that the incident was too bizarre to anticipate and protect against.

NOTE: It is important to realize that lack of knowledge of the threat in and of itself may not be a sufficient reason to validate a foreseeability determination of "not-foreseeable."   In truth, foreseeability is concerned not only with that which an Innkeeper knows *but what he should have known.* It is a takeoff on the old legal cliche that ignorance of the law is no excuse.

Knowledge of the level of foreseeability should be examined. There are a multitude of ways in which an Innkeeper can and must be kept abreast of the threats and their foreseeability which exist in and around his property. He can engage in informal conversations with the local beat police representative. He may hold more formal meetings, either intermittent or scheduled and documented with the police precinct officials, or attend scheduled meetings of the local chamber of commerce or the local Innkeepers association.

LOW FORESEEABILITY

Low foreseeability is defined as that level of threat which, after considering the three ingredient factors (premises, crime demographics, location) a thoughtful and reasonable person *and the Innkeeper* would not anticipate the threat to occur on the property. Such a determination would be based on the absence of previous similar incidents during the past two or three years, and incidents preceding that period would be too statistically remote to apply. These considerations would be given additional weight by an absence of fear of the incident by guests and/or sensitive employees.

MODERATE FORESEEABILITY

Moderate foreseeability is defined as that level of threat which, after considering the three ingredient factors (premises, crime demographics, and location) a thoughtful and reasonable person *and the Innkeeper* would anticipate the possibility of threat occurring. Such a determination would be based on only a limited number of previous such incidents over the past several years, and what appears to be no identifiable pattern or trend. These conditions would be given additional weight by only an average amount of awareness and fear on the part of guests and/or sensitive employees.

HIGH FORESEEABILITY

High foreseeability is defined as that level of threat which, after considering the three ingredient factors (premises, crime demographics, and location) a thoughtful and reasonable person *and the Innkeeper* would actually anticipate that the incident would occur. Such a determination would be based on a pattern of various incidents at that property and in the surrounding area for the previous several years.

The prior number of incidents would statistically suggest a high probability of continued incidents if radical protection management measures were not implemented.

The property might show signs of vandalism and disrepair. The surrounding area might show evidence of such protection management attempts such as bars on the windows, alarm boxes, and perimeter fences. These conditions would be given additional weight by an elevated fear of incidents on the part of guests and/or sensitive employees. High police patrol efforts and the feeling of local police officials might well be negative at the property and in the surrounding neighborhoods.

SUMMARY OF REASONABLE CARE AND FORESEEABILITY

We have determined that reasonable care is decreed as the standard of care that we must provide to our guests. Further, we have explored how such a level may be determined and have concluded that while the "reasonable person" test is most often quoted, the adage that "reasonable care is what the jury decides it is" is the most helpful. That approach will guide us through this text.

We have also seen that "foreseeability" is a major ingredient in reasonable care and have identified the various levels of foreseeability which range from non-foreseeability to high foreseeability.

Our understanding of these ranges and a sensitivity to the level of crime foreseeability on our property is the first step in establishing and maintaining reasonable care.

POINTS TO PONDER

THE LAWS AFFECTING THE LODGING INDUSTRY

◆   Identify the five "ingredients" which generally must be in place for an Innkeeper to be held liable for an incident involving an injury to a guest.

◆   Discuss, from that list of five, which two are most meaningful to the Innkeeper and about which he should be most concerned.

◆   Discuss what is meant by the term "foreseeability" insofar as the Innkeeper is concerned.

◆   Discuss means by which the Innkeeper may determine crime foreseeability with respect to his property.

◆   Discuss why raw crime statistics may be unreliable for the purpose of determining foreseeability.

◆   Discuss the importance of an Innkeeper knowing the levels of crime foreseeability at and surrounding his property.

EXECUTIVE SUMMARY OF PART TWO

HOTEL PROTECTION MANAGEMENT

Part two of Hotel Protection Management is, in fact, the very HEART of this text.

We have seen in earlier chapters that the courts, having evolved over the past several centuries from English Common Law, do require that we as hoteliers provide "reasonable care" to our guests.

The next three chapters will explore basic management models and techniques concerning how such care may be initiated.

We will examine the step-by-step approach by which an Innkeeper may isolate, identify, and qualify those assets which he needs to protect, first and foremost being the guest. We will discuss how he may uncover and evaluate the various threats which exist to those assets, select appropriate countermeasures which reduce the likelihood of those threats occurring, and finally establish within his overall property management efforts, an integrated schedule of management science-based practices which insure the development of Reasonable Care.

In this process, we will see how the management considerations of both responsibility and accountability discussed in chapter two come into play and how the application of such considerations will allow not only the virtual assurance of reasonable care but also its successful continuation.

CHAPTER FOUR

PROTECTION MANAGEMENT MATRIX

In chapter two the proposition was advanced that the term "security" had outlived its usefulness and should be discarded and replaced with the term "protection." This contention is worth further explanation and justification.

To illustrate one of the basic problems with use of the term "security," consider the following scenario:

> A potential hotel guest telephones a major resort to inquire about reservations for himself and his family. During the dialogue with the reservations clerk, the caller asks the question, "Do you have security on the property?"

It would be not uncommon--perhaps almost expected--for the reply from the desk clerk to be something on the order of, "Yes, we have uniformed security guards every night from 10 p.m. until 6.a.m."

Perhaps from the clerk's standpoint, his answer was adequate. Thinking that the question concerned itself totally and exclusively with security guards his response was limited to that aspect of protection.

What the guest might have been asking, however, (and what the clerk failed to address) may have included the following:

> "Will my family be transported safely from the airport to the resort by a competent and experienced driver?"

> "Will our luggage be protected while I'm registering?"

"Will the bell staff safely escort me and my family to our room, and will the bellperson explain to me all the 'security' devices therein?"

"Will I be told what we are expected to do if an alarm should activate?"

"How may we secure our room by double-locking the door?"

"May I be assured that the guestroom key which I will be issued has not been duplicated and is not in the hands of an unauthorized employee or (more frighteningly) in the hands of a criminal?"

The list of possible concerns that the guest might have goes on and on, whether or not he asks them specifically and individually. But obviously none of these concerns would be addressed when he was assured that, "Yes, we have uniformed security."

What this imaginary scenario is meant to illustrate, again, is one of the basic tenants of this text: The term "security" is both ill-defined (perhaps non definable) and counterproductive because of its limited and limiting connotations.

The challenges and opportunities of the lodging industry, in the marketplace, are as clear, evident, and available as they ever have been. The threat of unfair competition, the threat of an unavailable capital sources, the threat of market downsizing--remain more or less constant. Success or failure in meeting those threats can lead to great success, at one extreme, or into business failure at the other.

As serious as these many threats are, however, they are neither the major threats we face, nor the threats about which we concern ourselves in this text. Those threats are embedded in the fear that is found, in some quarters of the lodging industry, that the marketplace is being replaced by the courtroom as the location where hotel success or failure is realized.

The lodging industry cannot hope to achieve the level of guest protection which the courts have imposed upon it without having viable, proven concepts and tools upon which to build a systemized, successful, and <u>legally defendable</u> program for guest protection <u>throughout the property</u>.

Such tools must be workable and easily manipulated to conform to each property's individual requirements. While the term "security" does not support or lend itself to such a property-wide process, the term "protection" certainly does. Thus, we have the need and the requirement to afford protection for our guests.

With that in mind, we will begin to examine the proactive aspects of hotel protection management.

Both theoretical and practical in the beginning, our focus will be on the tools, concepts, and models of guest protection as they interact with one another and are integrated into overall property management.

FOUR-PHASED APPROACH

Four phases constitute the underpinnings of our entire approach to the provision of guest protection. Built on the basic canon that **guest protection is an absolute requirement**, they are:

I   Identifying and examining the assets which an Innkeeper must protect

II   Identifying and examining threats to which these assets are exposed

III   Developing countermeasures which minimize those threats

IV   Integrating the resulting guest-protection profile into the entire property-management scheme

From this four-phased approach will emerge the developments of an effective program of guest protection which, once implemented, will allow the Innkeeper the comfort of knowing that it is in place and ongoing.

It should be noted that this theory and practice termed "protection management" is not limited to the lodging industry. On the contrary, the four-phased approach to protection (remember, we used to call it "security") works well in virtually any industry group. As an example, we will focus on a hypothetical high-tech electronics facility, with its considerable protection requirements, and then see how the specifics of the approach can easily be extrapolated to apply to the ownership and management of lodging establishments. Consider this possible example:

Phase I   Identifying and examining the assets to be protected.

In any given high-tech manufacturing and production facility, assets which require protection will most certainly include the products, proprietary production processes, highly confidential technological research-and-development procedures, and of course, the buildings, equipment, furnishings, and that all-important, highly trained, virtually irreplaceable assets, **the employees**.

When visualizing this protection approach, it is important to realize that these assets, collectively and individually, are *unique to this facility*. They differ in importance, in priority, in scope, and in description from the assets of any other facility. Even a duplicate facility on the other side of the street will have somewhat different assets.

We will discover that this is also true and of vital concern when we consider our hotel assets.

>Phase II   Identifying and examining the threats to which the assets are exposed.

Looking again at our example of the high-tech facility and considering the assets which have been identified above, one would consider that threats to those assets would include product theft, industrial espionage, fire exposure to the buildings, and accidents or crimes against persons. It is absolutely vital that one remember that when identifying these threats, they are as unique to this location as the assets are. So will they be with our hotel threats.

>Phase III   Developing Countermeasures which minimize those threats.

It follows naturally that once the assets and threats to them have been identified, the manager must embark on the process of identifying those particular, individually selected countermeasures, which are *specifically* designed to minimize the *specifically identified* threats to which those *specifically identified* assets are exposed.

>Phase IV   Integrating the resulting guest protection profile into the entire property-management scheme.

To complete this approach to protection management, the manager must then integrate his specifically selected countermeasures into his overall property-management scheme, and establish accepted management-science umbrellas over them. He will then assign responsibility, demand accountability, and establish training and continuity.

At this point, the lodging manager can be said to have begun the establishment of protection management.

"Simple and self-evident," it is easy to say. And that is correct; it should be both. Yet there are several major, real-world problems which present themselves when such an all-encompassing (and often-considered radical) approach to management is attempted. Please note:

* In all industry groups, managers often have a built-in bias against "security." (There's that word again.) They find it uncomfortable to accept and difficult to deal with. And, of course, they often fear the issue of expense.

* Managers often have difficulty accepting "security" (protection) on the same management terms and at the same management level as other functional management endeavors such as sales, production, transportation, housekeeping, etc.

* Managers, particularly in the lodging industry--even when and if they accept the requirements and necessity for protection--often fail to realize that such protection must be property-wide and property-specific.

Any and all of these dispositions manifest themselves when the lodging manager is faced with the challenge of guest protection. Most often, he is burdened with outdated thinking and the shortsighted and limiting usage of what is known as "security." He has been too long exposed to traditional thinking which holds--unfortunately and often tragically--to the mind set which leads him to consider protection only *after* a crime has occurred. Sadly and usually expensively, that is too late.

And because of outmoded thinking, what is the solution most often considered when reacting to a protection problem? "Add another guard." If it ever worked, that stale approach was weak at best, and it is woefully inadequate and counterproductive today.

It is inadequate because it is reactive. It is counterproductive because random countermeasure selection either invariably will bring about too much protection or, worse, result in too little protection.

The selection of particular countermeasures (often NOT a security guard), must come only after a systematic and thorough analysis of the first two considerations (phases), which are (1) the assets which need protection, and (2) the threats against which those assets must be protected.

Given the fact that each property is unique, it follows that the protection scheme designed to protect such an entity against threats which also are unique to the property, must be unique. This individuality must be taken into consideration long before plans are formulated as to what types of protection to apply. (Phase III)

Different cities, different neighborhoods within the same cities, even different locations within the same neighborhood have different threats.

Different styles of building construction (e.g., high-rise versus garden variety) invite different threats.

Different construction, different furnishings and different employees all impact to produce different threats. The high-tech plant discussed earlier would require, for example, a different protection profile if it were located in a high-crime, urban slum area, as opposed to the exact duplicate facility located in a low-crime, low population, well-protected rural setting.

So, too, are our *assets* unique. Our guests--that number one asset which we are setting out to protect--are as unique both individually and collectively as are our properties, and as such, require unique protection. For example: If a property caters to a young, high-energy clientele, then it is obvious that the protection profile we seek must differ from that which we would establish if our clientele consisted primarily of senior citizens. We might well pay attention to proper liquor-serving training in the former, and pay more attention to slip-and-fall protection in the latter.

To expand this example, consider ingredients of a protection program we would establish if the property concentrated on business travel (principally Monday through Friday) versus the protection profile we would expect in a property catering to weekend vacation stays.

Given, then, the uniqueness of both the assets and the threats (the guests, in this instance, and the exposures they face), it follows that only after an analysis of both should the means of protection be decided.

This approach is facilitated by an extremely useful protection-management model. It is called a **Protection Management Matrix**. Diagraming it from the theory outlined above will portray the steps to be considered in the establishment of hotel protection management.

Figure 4-1 shows the protection management matrix. The horizontal plane shows space for the identifying of assets, and the vertical plane indicates the identified threats.

FIGURE: 4-1   PROTECTION MANAGEMENT MATRIX

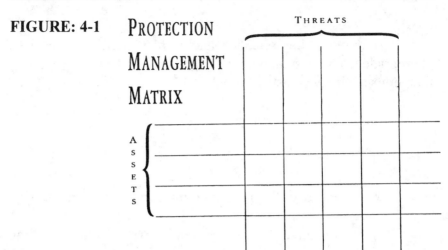

The blocks which are created by the intersection of the two planes offer space for the inclusion of those countermeasures which are determined to be appropriate to protect a particular asset from a particular threat.

This is obviously a simplistic graphic--where complexity is neither appropriate nor desired. A completed protection management matrix would show, on the horizontal plane, all the main assets--products, people, equipment, vehicles, etc. On the vertical plane it would list all of the major threats--such as lightning strikes, arson, theft, accidents, etc.

Finally, the entire spectrum of available countermeasures would be listed in the boxes outlined by the intersecting lines, showing all the countermeasures designed to eliminate, reduce, or provide quick response to each of the identified threats to each of the identified assets.

This development of a protection-management matrix is especially appropriate from the standpoint of our lodging industry. Repeating the points again, we must:

I   Identify our assets,

II   Identify our threats,

III   Identify all appropriate countermeasures, and, finally,

IV   Integrate our completed matrix into our overall property-management philosophy and practice.

THE ASSETS

Within the lodging industry, it can be said that there are three main assets to be protected.

FIRST AND FOREMOST IS THE GUEST

The guest comes to our property with certain expectations, and our ability to meet those expectations is directly related both to his subsequent decision to return and to our ultimate success. One prime expectation with which he comes--albeit perhaps subconsciously--is protection. The guest expects protection. He deserves protection. And the courts have held time and time again that *he has a right to protection, and we are charged with providing it.*

Every knowledgeable hotelier should know how absolute and critical such vital protection must be. All other considerations, literally, must come only after protection of the guest is addressed. It is possible for a property to survive with less-than-adequate food service (indeed, all too many do!), and it may survive with lounge facilities that are less than ideal. But no property, NO PROPERTY, can survive without its number one asset, the guest. Appropriately, then, the guest gets placed on the initial horizontal line of our protection matrix model.

Figure 4-2 shows the protection management matrix with the inclusion of the first asset--the guest.

FIGURE: 4-2

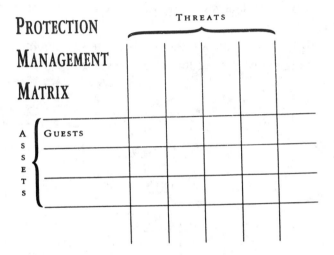

THE EMPLOYEE

In terms of value, the lodging industry's second most important asset (nearly as important as the guest) is the employee. Our obligation to protect our employees is, for the most part, steeped in a different set of legalities from those which come into play when we consider protection for our guests.

In addition to civil courts, where requirements dictate reasonable care for the guest, we are guided and directed with regard to employees by federal and state health and safety laws, along with such dictates as anti-discrimination and anti-harassment statutes, to name but a few.

In later chapters we will examine the proposition that the employee, an asset, if ill-chosen, ill-managed, ill-motivated and/or resentful and angry, can become a serious threat to another vital asset, the guest.

It follows, then, that not only must exceptional care be taken in the initial selection of employees, but then, once that high-quality work force is assembled, it must be protected. The employee, then, takes its proper place as the number two asset on the matrix.

Figure 4-3 shows the protection management matrix with the inclusion of the second asset--the employee.

FIGURE: 4-3

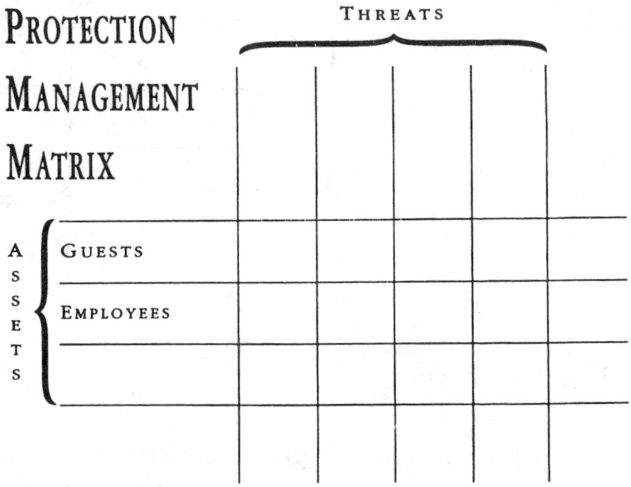

PROTECTION MANAGEMENT MATRIX

THREATS

ASSETS { GUESTS / EMPLOYEES

PHYSICAL ASSETS OF THE PROPERTY

The third asset for which the Innkeeper is responsible, and toward which he must direct protection, is actually a collection of assets--the physical, hard, valuable items which are vital to our continued success. They include the property structures guestroom and office contents (FF&E), vehicles, monies, food and beverage, supplies, etc. While there may be, and commonly is, great monetary value represented by these physical assets, they rank only a distant third in

70

the pecking order of assets to be protected. This assertion is based on one simple but vital fact: any physical asset, no matter how valuable, can be insured and can be replaced. Lives, on the other hand--both guests and employees--are absolutely priceless and irreplaceable.

Figure 4-4 shows the completion of the horizontal planes with the addition of the final asset--the physical assets of the property.

FIGURE: 4-4

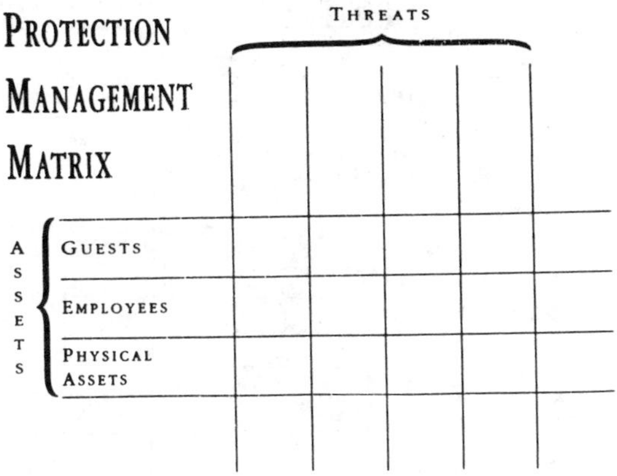

PROTECTION MANAGEMENT MATRIX

THREATS

ASSETS

GUESTS

EMPLOYEES

PHYSICAL ASSETS

While this appears obvious in the abstract, how many properties concentrate on protecting "things" rather than "people." They routinely conduct extensive pre-employment verification (background checks) on applicants who are being considered for, say, controllers or accountants (remember, they protect only money) while failing to do anywhere near such an extensive background verification on the likes of a room attendant applicant, or a potential bellperson. <u>And then we give virtually free access to our number one asset--the guest-- to such persons</u>!

To review, we have established, thus far, that while there are three major assets which we, as Innkeepers, must protect, there must be universal agreement that the guest is all-important. Without the guest, we would have no business.

We have seen on our developing matrix that the three assets are exposed to four threats. We will now identify and later examine and prioritize those threats.

Matrix Figure 4-5 shows the completed protection management matrix with all four of the threats identified on the vertical plane.

FIGURE: 4-5

PROTECTION MANAGEMENT MATRIX	THREATS					
	CRIME	FIRE	ACCIDENT	INJURY	NATURAL	DISASTER
ASSETS GUESTS						
EMPLOYEES						
PHYSICAL ASSETS						

THREATS

(1)   Fire, without doubt, is our biggest fear; its possibly catastrophic impact on us boggles the imagination. Fire is life threatening, property threatening and industry-threatening.

(2)   Accident and Injuries may be nearly as serious as fire.

(3)   Natural disaster, examples of which we view through the media, can literally obliterate cities and town.

Should not any of these three threats be the focus of our protection concerns? The answer is, "No."

(4)   *Crime is the threat upon which we will focus throughout this text*   A very brief examination of the first three threats will explain this rationale.

Fire: It is probably safe to say that the lodging industry has enjoyed a reasonable and sometimes exemplary history of combating fire. While the tragedy of spectacular hotel fires splashes across the headlines, statistically speaking such occurrences are not common. We are blessed with strong fire codes and easily accessible resources. From our local fire authorities to the National Fire Association, guidance and assistance in combating this threat are readily available.

Accidents and Injuries: To a large degree this threat, too, is well managed within the lodging industry. Guidance, direction and assistance have long been available. The Innkeeper has but to turn to OSHA or his insurance carrier for such help.

Natural Disaster: Assistance in combating this threat, too, is readily available. The National Weather Service, local emergency agencies, and Federal Emergency Management Agency (FEMA) are willing and able to provide guidance and information.

But what of crime?

Since we have already discovered that police agencies are not in the business of crime prevention, where can we turn for assistance? And as shown above, help is available with regard to all three of the other threats.

But what of crime?

Where can help, assistance and guidance be obtained when we attempt to neutralize this threat? After the following discussion of the first three threats, the remainder of this chapter will identify the concepts that will provide this greatly needed and much sought after help.

THE THREATS

FIRE

Many readers, particularly those who are traditional hotel security practitioners, may express surprise and opposition to "fire" being identified not only as the principal threat, but moreover may object to the subject even being identified as a "security" concern. To any reader with such a predisposition, please recall that early in chapter one we discussed the fact that this is not a "security" text but rather it concerns itself with "protection," specifically Hotel Protection. Within that context, any physical threat to our assets is an appropriate concern.

In terms of potential devastating loss, fire is without question the greatest single threat which our industry faces. It happened that the author was standing on the roof of an adjoining casino when the MGM Grand Hotel and Casino in Las Vegas burned. The devastating loss of life, the misery and pain, the terrible financial, professional and personal losses which ensued are images not soon forgotten. We will not, however, devote great time to this threat.

ACCIDENTS AND INJURIES

Like fire, the threat of accidents and injuries will not be discussed in great detail within this text. It is, without a doubt, a major concern, and constitutes the potential for extreme personal and financial loss. This text, however, will not delve into the details of how to inform your maintenance workers not to stand on the very top of a step ladder, nor remind you to advise your guests to be careful not to attempt to walk through the sliding glass doors leading to the balconies outside their rooms.

But accidents and injuries are serious threats, nonetheless, and like fire, can be significantly diminished through the diligent application of *hotel protection management* approaches.

NATURAL DISASTER

The third threat which the Innkeeper and, indeed, the entire lodging industry faces, is that of natural disaster. It is the prime example that justifies the premise that in hotel protection management planning, *universal "security standards" are suspect and that each property protection plan must be individualized and unique unto itself.*

There are certain professional protection practitioners (fortunately few in number) who argue with this point. They insist that standards of protection (security standards, if you will) are needed and long overdue for the entire lodging industry. This position is absolute folly--exemplified perfectly by the threat of natural disaster.

Even if several facilities were designed by the same architect and constructed by the same builders, the properties would be unique unto themselves. As such there is an absolute, basic requirement that *the protection profile established for each property must also be unique.*

What "standard of protection" would possibly be appropriate, for instance, for a tidal wave alert system in Tucson, Arizona? Or a heavy snowstorm warning system in Tahiti? Should a property manager concern himself with river flooding at a mountaintop resort? Or an avalanche on a coastal beach? Only if the end of the world is at hand.

Of the four major threats with which we must concern ourselves, natural disaster is, obviously, the one most difficult to deter. In fact, it is impossible. The protection management aim with regard to treating this threat, unlike the other three threats, is *not* proactive. By necessity, it must be *reactive*, although the planning, as all other planning, must be before the fact.

Such protection plans must call for identification of the natural disasters which are possible, or likely, in our own particular geographic area (hurricanes, floods, windstorms, etc.) It is then necessary to plan for the possibility and likelihood of their occurrence, and prepare our staffs in appropriate responses.

CRIME

Is there a subject anywhere more written about than crime? As much is written, and discussed, about crime than perhaps any other subject.

We read of crime against the elderly, against juveniles, against spouses.

We hear about crime as it affects us financially.

We hear about crime as it affects us morally.

We hear about crime as it affects us professionally.

Our guests, and to a somewhat lesser degree, our employees, face at all times the threat of crime--literally from the moment they set foot on the property. And, in cases of properties which operate airport vans, they face this threat *before* they even enter the property.

Next to fire, crime is the threat which we, as hoteliers, fear most--and for good reason. Fire is all-encompassing, terrifying, life-threatening and totally devastating. Crime can be equally disastrous. It can strike with silent suddenness while the remaining occupants of the property are totally unaware. To its victim, it can be devastating. And unlike what is said of lightning, it *can* strike twice. The second strike comes in the courts.

Given all the press, the discussion, the studies and concerns, one would think that if we, as a society, had a handle on *any* issue, that issue would be crime. Apparently this is not so. Despite all the attention and research on the subject, it is fair to say that we know all too little about it.   The basic and overriding reason for this is _we do not know what the root cause of crime is, if indeed one exists_.

One political faction in our society holds that crime, with all its growth, is a result of a criminal justice system which fails to deliver swift, sure, and severe penalties for having committed crime. Diametrically opposed is the strong vocal, political viewpoint which holds that crime is fostered by that same criminal justice system which is *too* severe. And rather than placing convicted criminals into overcrowded, crime-breeding prisons, society should be investing in rehabilitation.

Then there are those who argue that education is the answer to crime, and it is the lack thereof which causes crime. If this is true, how can we account for the white-collar criminal who has college degree, after degree, after degree, but who still commits crime?

There are those who say that full employment is the answer to crime, and the lack thereof is the root cause. If this is true, how can we explain the well-employed accountant who commits embezzlement against his own employer?

Others say that spiritual values are the answer, and the lack of such a value system provides the foundation for crime. How, then, do we account for the cleric, who commits outrageous acts against children in his parish?

Families and family values, according to some, are the answers. To others, a more even distribution of wealth is necessary before crime can be eradicated.

The list of supposed causes and solutions is as long and varied as the list of self-proclaimed experts who claim to know all the answers. Where does the truth actually lie? It is probably safe to say that no one knows for certain. It is also probably safe to say that any or all of the possible reasons listed significantly impact on both the causes and growth of crime. Further it is probably equally safe to say that proper, well-funded and carefully monitored social adjustments could present possible solutions.

None of these, again, is the single answer.

The solution to the crime problem eludes us despite claims of politicians at every level, that their pet "crime bill" will magically rescue the populace from the grip and fear of crime.

We as a society have not discovered a single root cause for crime and therefore it can be effectively argued that without knowing the cause(s) of crime (to the extent that we know the causes of fire, the causes of accidents and the causes of severe weather) we are unable to develop a *certain cure or prevention for crime.*

And yet, as Innkeepers, it is essential to remember that not only must we protect our guests from crime, but remember too, that little or no help is forthcoming from tax-based resources. For the most part, we are on our own.

Why, given the seemingly endless amount of tax dollars we have spent on anti-crime bills, on correctional facilities, on police protection, can we not be protected? Why are we "on our own?"

Given the community, the county, the state, and the national police resources, why must we as Innkeepers bear the burden of crime prevention on our properties?

The answer is possibly a shocker to some, and heresy to others. It is that police know no more than the rest of us, about the causes of crime. Indeed, for the most part they are **not in the business of preventing crime.**

This assertion begs explanation.

If , indeed, police do not "do" crime prevention, then what do they do? The answer is simple and straightforward. They do exactly what their bosses (you and I and all other taxpayers) require them to do. As we discussed in chapter two:

*   They respond to emergencies
*   They investigate
*   They interrogate
*   They incarcerate
*   And they testify in court.

In a summation, they attempt not to prevent crime, but only to solve one after it has been committed.

Police do respond. They do investigate, interrogate, and all those other good things. They do their best, often under the worst of conditions, to address crime--but only after it has been committed. They merely react.

We **(Innkeepers)** in the private sector, on the other hand, must address crime proactively. If crime is to be deterred and reduced and since as we have seen above, no one including the police is equipped or budgeted for crime prevention, it falls on us to accomplish the task.

CRIME PREVENTION

In the face of all previous assertions that crime is not preventable, it seems incongruous to present an entire section on "crime prevention." This is not, however, as contradictory as it may seem.

The claim that crime cannot be prevented means that specific crime as a broad, general category cannot be prevented. There is considerable evidence to back up this assertion. Despite studies, research, massive funding and education, it appears that society cannot broadly, prevent *crime*. And if indeed, crime can be prevented society has yet to find the ability to do so.

This is not meant to imply that a *single* crime cannot be deterred, or perhaps even totally prevented.

It can. **And we must learn to do it.**

A theory of crime prevention can be simply and effectively demonstrated by using other previously identified threats in analogous and specific models. Let's begin with the analogy of another major hotel threat, that of fire, ignoring crime prevention for the moment. Let's look at how fire prevention is theorized and practiced.

For comparative and illustrative purposes, we begin with a basic explanation of fire. In order to become a physical phenomenon, fire must have three ingredients, often depicted as the "fire triangle." Figure 4-6 depicts that fire triangle.

FIGURE: 4-6

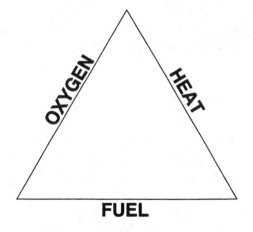

FIRE TRIANGLE

Fire requires oxygen.

Fire requires fuel.

And fire requires heat.

When either fighting fire or preventing it, it must be recognized that all three legs of the triangle are necessary ingredients. Without them, a fire can neither occur, nor survive.

Oxygen. If oxygen can be eliminated, the fire is extinguished. One effective means is to use a CO_2 (carbon dioxide) extinguisher. The chemicals in the extinguisher displace the oxygen surrounding the fire and it cannot continue to burn. Smothering a fire with a blanket is another example.

Fuel. Fire just doesn't burn in the abstract; it requires fuel. Eliminating fuel will successfully extinguish the fire. An obvious example of this in firefighting practice is the cutting of a fire line in the face of an advancing forest fire. Fire fighters purposely burn, or otherwise clear, an area in front of the oncoming fire so that when it reaches that point, there will be no fuel upon which it can feed itself, and it will burn out.

Heat. By lowering the temperature—using water, for instance —the fire can be brought under control.

Using any, or a combination, of the three necessary ingredients, a fire can be suppressed. Or avoided.

But what of the crime fighter? (And the Innkeeper?) While this is arguably a much more difficult task, a triangle, again, is an effective model.

Figure 4-7 shows the crime triangle. Like the fire triangle it is a graphic display for the ingredients generally necessary for crime. Each leg--**motive, ability and opportunity**, is a required element in order for the crime to be committed.

FIGURE: 4-7

CRIME TRIANGLE

To examine these three components and understand the workings of the triangle, let's consider a hypothetical hotel burglary.

Motive. The perpetrator of the crime of room burglary will have, obviously, a motive. Usually, it is financial--steal something of value that can be turned into cash. Perhaps to satisfy a drug habit. Or because of illness in his family. Even to pay off a debt to the IRS. Then again, he may simply be greedy or lazy, and decide that his basic living needs are best fulfilled by committing this crime. It is possible, also, that he is simply anti-social, with a twisted mental orientation and that the motive for room burglary is a psychological one.

Whatever the motive, whatever the "need," if we could remove it, we could eliminate the crime.

Ability. This leg of the crime triangle is probably the most obvious: a room burglar must have the ability to do that task. He cannot commit the crime on mental state alone; some physical action is necessary.

He must have, for instance, the combined mental and physical abilities to place himself in the vicinity of the guestroom. He must have the ability to move himself into the room, then to seize and steal its valuable contents. The abilities seem to be minimal, but they are, nonetheless, vital. To cite an extreme for the sake of demonstration, a bedridden paraplegic probably does not have the ability to commit this crime.

Thus ability, like motive, is a necessary ingredient in crime and like motive, if we could eliminate ability, we could eliminate the crime.

Opportunity. Finally, the room burglar must have the opportunity to commit the crime. He must be afforded the opportunity to move, unchallenged, to the target which is the guest room; the opportunity to gain entrance into the room, to collect whatever booty, and then depart unchallenged.

Thus we have the third leg of the crime triangle, joined to motive and ability.

OPPORTUNITY is unique in that it is <u>the only component which we can affect</u>.

Recalling the fire triangle for a moment, it was noted that by removing any of the three elements--oxygen, fuel, or heat--the firefighter may expect a reasonable degree of success. But while <u>consistent with the fire triangle in construction, only one leg of the crime triangle is available for the crime fighter (and the Innkeeper) to attack</u>.

To combat crime, the Innkeeper has no control over *motive*. Sociologists and psychologists often use this leg of the triangle to explain crime. Likewise, there is nothing he can do about *ability*. Chalk up another leg of the triangle to the advantage of the criminal.

That leaves the crime fighter (the Innkeeper in this case) only the one leg of the three-sided enemy to attack. But remember, if you pull out one leg of a tripod, the whole thing will collapse; so that's the one to go after: **opportunity**. It's the one aspect with which we can be expected to afford "reasonable care" toward the protection of our guests from crime. Remove the opportunity, and you eliminate the crime.

Eliminating (or reducing) the opportunity is a prime focus of Hotel Protection Management.

Remember what we continue to preach, that each property is unique unto itself. If yours has a unique exposure to the opportunity of crime, then you, as Innkeeper, must develop a unique method of protection against it. If expert attention from the outside is required, then you are well advised to seek it.

Remember that crime prevention theory, and practice, are no secrets, and they contain no magical formulas. In fact, many such theories and practical techniques that are quite useful to the Innkeeper have been developed, taught, and utilized with great success for years.

The National Crime Prevention Institute at the University of Louisville, for instance, began teaching individuals and police departments with notable success in the 1970s. During an era in which the Law Enforcement Assistance Administration (LEAA) was active at the federal level, significant amounts of tax dollars were funneled into municipal police agencies in order to teach the precepts and practices of crime prevention. Once that agency ceased to exist, and funding became a problem, proactive crime prevention was de-emphasized.

Since that time, it can be said that law enforcement at all levels has declined to invest sufficient amounts of their budget dollars in *prevention*. That necessary endeavor has now become not only the principal *domain*, but also the principal *responsibility* of the private sector. And that means, in our case, the Innkeeper.

It is the Innkeeper who is responsible for crime prevention on the property.

It is the Innkeeper who is charged with preventing acts of violence to his guest.

It is the Innkeeper who has the duty to provide **reasonable care** by crime-prevention techniques.

Can he do this task effectively?

Yes, he can. And if he hopes to successfully run his property, he must.

POINTS TO PONDER

PROTECTION MANAGEMENT MATRIX

◆   Identify each of the three assets which the Innkeeper is required to protect.

◆   Identify each of the four threats to which these assets are exposed.

◆   Defend the position that both threats and assets are "property-unique."

◆   Describe and define the Protection Management Matrix.

◆   Defend the position taken in the text that three of the threats have historically received more concentrated attention than the remaining one.

◆   Defend the position that "crime cannot be prevented."

◆   Identify at least four tasks normally performed by police agencies as they "enforce."

◆   Describe the fire triangle and identify its three components.

◆   Describe the crime triangle and identify its three components.

◆   Identify the single component of the crime triangle over which the Innkeeper has control.

CHAPTER FIVE

COUNTERMEASURES

In the previous chapters, we have seen that the paramount consideration of an Innkeeper must be the protection of his guests.

We also have been introduced to the management model labeled the Protection Management Matrix. That model, not yet completed, portrays a horizontal plane depicting the assets which the Innkeeper must protect, and on the vertical plane the threats which exist to those assets.

In this chapter, we will begin to complete the matrix and fill in the blanks created where the vertical and horizontal planes intersect. We will fill those boxes with *countermeasures*--techniques and methods which protect that particular asset from the particular threat indicated. Our number one asset, once again, is our guest, and the threat which is our particular concern is crime.

Of the four threats to our guests, crime (at least the prevention thereof) receives the least attention from our tax-based support system. That leaves it as the single threat with which the Innkeeper must deal alone and independently, essentially without any public assistance. Given society's apparent inability to address this threat, this monumental task would seem to be beyond the realm of the Innkeeper's ability.

Fortunately, this is not the case.

Innkeepers can, and in fact, do what society apparently has been unable or unwilling to do. By following specific models, practices and guidelines, the Innkeeper can affect a major impact on that societal menace as it falls within their purview.

In this and succeeding chapters we will see that there are eight countermeasures against crime, the use of which will allow the Innkeeper to accomplish his obligation to protect the guest. The selection, application and maintenance of those eight countermeasures are economically feasible, as well as operationally feasible after the property has been appropriately surveyed by the Innkeeper.

Confidence that these eight countermeasures are in place and being addressed can be assured by the adoption and use of a management model which we call the Protection Management Matrix. This device will serve as a tool for the accomplishment of hotel protection management.

Discussed in the first chapter of this text was the fact that guest protection (remember, we used to call it "security") often has been a subject which the Innkeeper traditionally has mismanaged or failed to manage. It is a subject with which he has been traditionally uncomfortable.

Addressing those discomforts and fears, we shall find that we can reduce to a *total of eight* the seemingly endless possible approaches. Protection is neither steeped in some magical mystique nor is it difficult to achieve. On the contrary, as are all functions within the lodging industry, it is a discipline which can and *must be* learned, applied, and successful.

Our challenge, then, is to confront, head on, the issue of preventing specific crimes to our number one asset, our guests. Our next step in accomplishing this task is understanding the eight countermeasures which can be placed in our Protection Management Matrix. These countermeasures include:

(1)   Pre-employment verification techniques

(2)   Guest Protection Training

    (3)   Access control

    (4)   Lighting

    (5)   Key control

    (6)   Protection officers

    (7)   Guestroom protection

    (8)   Emergency responses

There are those who will argue that this list of only eight guest protection countermeasures ignores traditional mechanical/electrical methods such as alarm devices. By their nature and character, however, those devices fit as a subset into the countermeasures of *Guestroom protection, Access control or Emergency response.*

COUNTERMEASURE ONE

PRE-EMPLOYMENT VERIFICATION

Tradition might hold that pre-employment verification (often known as background checking) is a function exclusive to Human Resources, and not something with which an Innkeeper should be concerned as a guest-protection technique. Not so. In fact, it may be the *single most important, most effective, and least expensive* countermeasure technique available to the Innkeeper for provision of guest protection and reasonable care.

Why should this be so? The reason is simple.

> It has been estimated with reliability and replication that at least 85 percent of protection incidents (including crime) that occur on a given property, involve *employees.*

This may shock and dismay the reader but it is a condition about which every lodging industry employee should be cognizant.

The employee--that valued, necessary ingredient which we saw earlier on the protection management matrix--can be and often is a threat rather than an asset.

It is a sad truth which the lodging business shares with several other industries. Although there are no excuses for this condition, there are several explanations:

* Frequent and rapid turnover of employees
* Relatively low wages
* Propensity within the industry for ineffective personnel management
* And foremost: the failure, on the part of those persons responsible for hiring, to affect proper pre-employment verification techniques.

As discouraging as these truths are, the bright alternative is as simple as recognizing the several causes.   When properly introduced, applied and maintained, pre-employment techniques can and do facilitate extraordinary results.

* They reduce turnover significantly.
* They result in vastly improved staff morale.
* They decrease, astoundingly, the incidents of crime on the property.
* They act as effective, demonstrable, and impressive evidence of reasonable care if and when litigation is brought against the   property alleging inadequate guest protection.

Again, this is a countermeasure that is both inexpensive and highly effective. And contrary to some beliefs, it can be done legally, morally, and ethically.

COUNTERMEASURE TWO

STAFF-WIDE TRAINING

The inclusion, as a countermeasure, of such an apparently non-"security-related" subject as staff-wide training may raise as many eyebrows as did the inclusion of pre-employment verification. *There is, however, no more effective and no more all encompassing effort possible across the depth and breadth of the property than the training of the entire staff in the techniques of guest protection.*

Consider the following occurrences which caused extreme guest harm:

> A room attendant who spoke no English was at her first day on the job. She was approached by a fashionably dressed male who, through impromptu sign language, managed to convince her that he needed to get into a particular guest room which she assumed to be his. It was not. The actual guest in the room, an airlines flight attendant, was raped and seriously beaten. **The room attendant had not been trained in guest protection.**

> A front desk clerk was approached by a person asking for a guestroom key in order to "surprise my husband." She did, indeed. Her husband, who was entertaining another woman, was shot by the wife. **The desk clerk had not been trained in guest protection**.

An overly zealous room service employee (perhaps overly greedy) agreed to continue to supply a roomful of guests with order after order of alcohol. The guests turned out to be under age, and tragically, one died. **The room service employee had not been trained in guest protection**.

The list of tragic examples seems endless. Guest protection and reasonable care training in literally every department are essential. Training must be conducted upon initial hiring. It must be well constructed and documented, and it must continue throughout the tenure of the employee.

Not unlike the countermeasure of pre-employment verification, staff wide training has the multiple advantages of raising morale, raising efficiency, reducing turnover, and above all, it is an effective way to achieve reasonable care. And contrary to common thinking in the lodging industry, training need not be expensive.

COUNTERMEASURE THREE

ACCESS CONTROL

One countermeasure which is already in existence on virtually every lodging property is Access Control. Akin to many of our countermeasure controls, however, it has not been historically isolated, identified and managed as a single protection entity. It should be.

By definition, access control is that countermeasure which permits, denies, limits, controls or monitors pedestrian and vehicular traffic on, into and out of the property. It can be a significant countermeasure which reduces the likelihood of crime occurring to the guest as well as to the employee. It comes in several forms, designs and applications, depending upon the construction, location and design of the property to be protected.

It often begins, depending upon the property configuration, at the perimeter. On many properties, it consists of fencing, shrubbery or other physical constraints.

At the perimeter of the property, as well as along building perimeters, it is most often and most effectively used with the companion countermeasure of lighting.

Moving from the perimeter toward the centralized portions of the property, access control begins to take a multitude of forms.

It may consist of signs, which direct both pedestrians and vehicles to move, or act, or be restrained in a manner consistent with the wishes of the Innkeeper. Examples include speed-limit signs, limited-admittance signs, guest-assistance signs (i.e., restroom locations) and signs announcing hazardous warnings. Contrary to what many believe, signs *do* work. (E.g., Guests almost invariably pick the correct restrooms!)

Access control also consists of internal barriers and controls such as speed bumps, locked doors (not to be confused with key control, a countermeasure to follow), chains and other types of barricades for vehicular control, and flashing lights at construction or repair points.

NOTE: No countermeasure is absolutely foolproof. The term "access control," can be misleading. The word "control" suggests an absolute, which is a false premise. Access control is a *relative condition.* For maximum effectiveness, access control is normally used in conjunction with other related countermeasures such as key control and security officers.

COUNTERMEASURE FOUR

LIGHTING

It goes without saying that lighting is a countermeasure which is by no means unique to the lodging industry. It has been in use perhaps as long as man has attempted to counteract crime. Further, crime is not the only threat against which man has historically used lighting. He used it in the form of fire, for instance, to frighten away dangerous animals. It is, simply, a countermeasure which **works**--even against the dangerous, two-legged animals which lurk on and around our properties today.

It has been shown, statistically, that all crime is reduced when lighting is strategically and effectively employed.

Going hand-in-hand with access control, its significant baseline ingredients are: placement, focus and intensity.

Management challenges for the lighting countermeasure to crime are highlighted by the need for documented, consistent maintenance.

Generally, its greatest downside, unless properly engineered and planned-for early on, can be its cost.

Management ingredients for the effective use of lighting include:

* Parking lot applications
* Use in heavily traveled walkways
* Concentration on portal areas
* Integration of both interior and exterior usage
* Control and switch-box protection
* Emergency applications

COUNTERMEASURE FIVE

KEY CONTROL

This is among the most obvious countermeasures to crime. Unfortunately, the reverse is also true, and the lack of adequate key control--with monumental and often tragic results--has many times been the basis for a legal determination that guest protection and reasonable care were not in place.

There are those among the lodging industry, otherwise sophisticated hospitality managers, who doubt that key control is possible. They believe that control is impossible, given the numbers and types and movement of property keys. Unfortunately, they sometimes virtually disregard any attempt to manage effectively this countermeasure. Such thinking is not only invalid, it is dangerous.

Control of keys *is* possible. It is also *essential*.

With a myriad of keying and locking systems available, from mechanical to electronic, from cards of one construction to several others, the array of problems seems endless. However, one paramount fact remains constant. The Innkeeper must manage his system.

Despite claims by manufacturers and suppliers of the newest innovations in keying systems (particularly, of course, those designed for guestroom protection) no system is foolproof. No system can be relied upon to provide the expected protection at all times, and no system will remain secure *in the absence of system management by the manager*.

Generally speaking, key control can be categorized into at least two distinctive areas, guest room keys and back-of-the-house keys and may be divided into eight categories:

*   Requisition
*   Production
*   Storage
*   Transport
*   Control
*   Issuance
*   Retrieval
*   Inventory

Recoring, rekeying, and rotation are all of concern. All of these subjects will be addressed in greater length later in this text. Special significance will be noted of the necessity of protection of particularly sensitive keys, the E Key and others.

COUNTERMEASURE SIX

PROTECTION (SECURITY) OFFICERS

The term "protection officer" is significantly more appropriate to the lodging industry than that of "security officer." However, for the sake of clarity, the terms will be used interchangeably throughout this chapter.

Of primary concern is the "management" of this countermeasure. Historically, on their facilities, Innkeepers have placed security officers and then, like no other function on the property, left them virtually on their own. They have been historically and traditionally poorly selected, poorly managed, poorly equipped, poorly paid and what is most important, poorly regarded.

A considerable number of properties have elected to utilize this protection officer countermeasure and doubtless will continue to do so. It behooves the Innkeepers, then, to examine the worth, the expense, the proper application and the exposures thereof.

He needs to consider the following:

* Direct and indirect costs involved
* Types of security officers available
* Methods of recruitment
* Methods of training
* Methods of supervision
* Scope of responsibility
* The weapons decision
* Limits of duties and activities

The cost of using security officers as a countermeasure is extremely high--potentially the most expensive of all countermeasures. On the other hand, they can be and often are the most effective. If for no other reasons than these two, the use of security officers should be carefully weighed, carefully managed and carefully utilized.

COUNTERMEASURE SEVEN

GUESTROOM PROTECTION

The guest is more vulnerable to acts of criminality while within the guestroom than during any other time or at any other place on the property.

The reasons are apparent:

> The guest usually spends more time in the guestroom than any other location on the property. (That fact alone marks the guestroom as the location where the highest crime vulnerability exists.)

> The guest is often asleep, obviously, in this guestroom and this is another factor which increases vulnerability.

The time spent in the guestroom, for the most part, is during nighttime hours--times when traditionally hotel staffing numbers are at their lowest. This reduced staff level also adds to the guest's exposure.

And finally, nighttime itself statistically poses problems.

Viewed in this total context, it becomes apparent that considerable management care and thought must be focused on the guestroom itself. Guestroom protection, the seventh of the eight countermeasures, comes into play.

COUNTERMEASURE EIGHT

EMERGENCY RESPONSE PROCEDURES

Since the thrust of this text has been *prevention* (read that as proactive management) the inclusion of emergency response procedures as a countermeasure may seem a contradiction in terms. And perhaps it is. Even so, it has been held in court, time and time again, that while the deterrent to incidents against the guest is vital, it is considered equally important that the staff be prepared to *respond* to emergencies should they arise.

An effective emergency response program, not unlike other countermeasures, begins with the survey. Different, however, than the property survey during which we will examine the vulnerabilities and weaknesses in the protection profile, this survey is one of history.

The Innkeeper bent upon an effective emergency response program (and that should include all Innkeepers) should examine the history of events at and surrounding the property and consider what response could and should be expected. Such history includes analysis of:

* Severe weather
* Medical emergencies
* Fire emergencies
* Crime emergencies

The effective Innkeeper must plan for and train in anticipation of any or all of these conditions.

POINTS TO PONDER

COUNTERMEASURES

◆   Identify the eight countermeasures from which an Innkeeper may choose in order to develop or adjust a guest protection program.

◆   Briefly describe the content, value and applicability of each of the eight countermeasures.

◆   Select one countermeasure which you feel may be the most effective and defend your position.

CHAPTER SIX

THE PROTECTION MANAGEMENT SURVEY

We discovered in chapter five that there are eight ways to protect the guest from crime. There are eight countermeasures which, when appropriately applied, can act as effective deterrents to this major threat which faces our number one asset. Three questions come to the Innkeeper's mind when he considers the employment of these eight deterrents.

*   The seriousness and criticality of the threats

*   The countermeasures already in existence and their
        effectiveness and appropriateness

*   The need for new or adjusted countermeasures

There is but one known effective method which may be used to address these concerns. *The Innkeeper must survey his property.*

To the casual observer, this may seem a simple and reasonable course of action. If an Innkeeper is to "do" guest protection and reasonable care, he must survey his property. Simple and reasonable. To many Innkeepers, however, it is often considered an affront.

"Survey my property? Ridiculous! I know my property like the back of my hand! There isn't a nook or cranny about which I'm unfamiliar. No one knows this property as well as I do."

In truth, he is reluctant to admit, even to himself, that there might be conditions or activities or objects or (worst case) threats on the property about which he is unaware. And in truth, there almost invariably are!

Innkeepers, not unlike all overworked and extremely busy professionals, never seem to find the time to do some of the things they know in their hearts they should do. They get caught up in personnel and human resource problems. They get busy with maintenance emergencies. They are overloaded with paperwork.

The events which tax and capture the Innkeeper go on and on. And in the midst of those ever-present and often consuming pressures, he often does not remain "on top" of all the aspects of his property.

As much as he would like to know, for instance, how accessible his property is to "bad guys," something like payroll problems always seem to get his attention first.

As much as he would like to know if it's possible there is an ex-felon employed on the property, something like a major banquet and its problems always seems to get his attention first.

As much as he would like to know if his contract security officers are sleeping (or worse, stealing), (or worse yet, being a physical threat to the guests) something like franchise renewal contracts always seem to get his attention first.

He has fallen into the work-a-day trap and while the safety and security of his guests are important to him, he simply does not often give this subject proper time.

These, however, are "explanations" for lack of protection concern, not "excuses."

No matter how arduous the task might seem, no matter how familiar he believes he is with his property, no matter how much other work may pile up, he *must survey his property.*

He must survey it during daylight hours as well as at nighttime.

He must survey it during weekends as well as during weekdays.

He must survey it completely and systematically.

This systematic approach calls for a countermeasure-specific analysis utilizing a survey checklist which should be developed, unique to the property.   This systematic survey checklist is absolutely critical and has three purposes:

(1)   It is used by the GM as his initial roadmap. As a roadmap, it will guide him not only through each department but call his attention to protection-related countermeasures within that department.

(2)   It is used by the Protection Management Committee (covered in chapter seven) to evaluate the property's protection profile. This evaluation should be the result of that committee viewing collectively the survey check list initially prepared by the GM.

(3)   Finally it is used by the designated department head (shown in the Wagon Wheel, also covered in chapter seven.) It will act as a guideline tool for the establishment and maintenance of those countermeasures initiated by the protection management committee.

The importance of the survey and its three-pronged usage cannot be overemphasized.

THE SURVEY FORMAT

As indicated earlier, the initial step in the three-step survey approach should be done by the General Manager. There is little question that this is an arduous and difficult task but one which is vital if reasonable care is to be assured.

First and foremost it is a *diagnostic* process. It is designed first to gather facts and impressions and opinions, (accomplished by the GM.) The *remedial* process comes subsequently when the protection management committee and the designated department head become involved.

*   It is a process of walking, and perhaps driving when the property is so configured.

*   It is a process of observing.

*   It is a process of asking questions.

*   It is a process of completing a survey checklist.

*   It is a process of adding to or detracting from that checklist as the survey progresses.

*   It is a process which may take from several hours to several days depending on the size of the property.

It is a process steeped in the eight countermeasures with which that GM must be familiar.

The process begins with the GM developing the checklist specific to his own property. This checklist may be developed using the countermeasure guidelines which follow. He then can proceed to view his property systematically.

As he conducts the survey and completes the checklist, he should be neither judgmental nor subjective. Rather, he should attempt objective impartiality, even in the face of what initially may appear to be a protection problem.

When the survey results reach the protection management committee, a "weeding out" process is appropriate. Finally these adjusted results will be assigned to the appropriate Wagon Wheel department manager for suitable action.

The GM should complete the survey with simple written responses to each question: "Yes," "No," "Not applicable," or "Unknown." Again, no judgments on his part are proper at this time.

COUNTERMEASURE ONE

PRE-EMPLOYMENT VERIFICATION (PEV)

When preparing the checklist for this survey, it must be property-specific.

The following general survey/checklist items are usually applicable to most properties.

> Is there a written policy/guideline for pre-employment verification?
>
> Is there a system for monitoring, controlling, updating and enforcing this policy?
>
> Is there a policy in effect for hiring employees in an emergency situation, without subjecting those employees to PEV procedures?
>
> If so, are the required PEV procedures consistently followed up on, and is such follow-up enforced, monitored, and audited?
>
> Is there a system for monitoring, controlling, updating and enforcing this policy?

Has a single department (e.g., HR) been designated as the overall authority and responsible location for the conduct of PEV?

Have the PEV policies and guidelines and procedure been reviewed by counsel and is such review an ongoing process?

Has counsel reviewed the employment application form?

Irrespective of the designation of the overall property authority for PEV, does the head of the hiring department have ample input into the selecting and hiring process?

THE EMPLOYMENT APPLICATION FORM

Have hiring authorities (i.e., department heads) had training in employment application form review?

Does the application form have appropriate release from liability disclaimers and have such disclaimers been reviewed by counsel?

Is there a double check (both HR and the hiring department) to verify the completeness of the completed employment application form?

Does the employment application form address as appropriate and within correct legal guidelines the following subjects:

* Previous employment
* Previous experience
* Education
* References
* Credit history
* Criminal history
* Medical history

* Motor vehicle records
* Vital records

Does the PEV policy (as well as the instructions on the employment application form) require that each and every block be completed.

Does the employment application form clearly state that omissions or misrepresentations may be cause for job denial or subsequent termination?

Does the employment application clearly state that information provided by the applicant is subject to review?

THE INTERVIEW

Have hiring authorities been trained in interviewing techniques?

Have hiring authorities been trained in interviewing legalities?

Have they been trained specifically in what subjects are not to be addressed during the interview?

Does the interviewer carefully address the employment application in terms of completeness, applicability, and appropriateness?

THE VERIFICATION PROCESS

Does a written policy exist concerning the verification process?

Has counsel reviewed the verification process?

Has a specific department or position been designated as the authority responsible for the verification process?

Irrespective of this consideration, is the head of the hiring department afforded ample input into this process?

If appropriate and within the bounds of legality, are the following subjects from the employment application verified?

*   Previous employment
*   Previous experience
*   Education
*   References
*   Credit history
*   Criminal history
*   Medical history
*   Motor vehicle records
*   Vital records

COUNTERMEASURE TWO

GUEST PROTECTION TRAINING

A survey/checklist, aimed at staff-wide guest protection training, obviously concerns itself with all departments since the concept of property-wide guest protection training touches all departments.

The survey/checklist therefore will vary according to the property's approach to each department's involvement and level of training. A general survey/checklist approach, however, will often include the following:

Does a written guest protection training policy exist?

If so, does it include an overall property training objective and include all departments and all employees?

Is there a single property-wide training guideline showing which subjects are to be taught to which employees on what initial and recurring basis?

Are there directives which outline, for each department head, the methods and alternatives available for teaching?

Has the "trainer" in each department been properly trained, not only in the guest protection subject matter but in the training methods available and desired?

Are there provisions for retroactive training when an employee has been hired on an emergency basis?

Are there provisions for appropriate training when an employee is transferred or promoted?

Are appropriate guest protection issues mandated for training in each department? Specifically are there provisions in each department (sales, personnel, housekeeping, front desk, F&B, room, HR, etc.) for the training of:

(1)   Pre-employment verification
(2)   Guest protection training
(3)   Access control
(4)   Lighting
(5)   Key control
(6)   Protection officers
(7)   Guestroom protection
(8)   Emergency response

For reemphasis, is each department required to conduct training in each countermeasure?

If so, is this summary periodically reviewed for compliance and timeliness?

Has a single person been designated to insure that all appropriate guest protection subjects are being taught?

Are there provisions for training upon initial employment followed by the requirement for periodic, scheduled and documented in-service training?

Is documentation of all training required?

Is such training documentation maintained either by the HR department or in another designated location?

COUNTERMEASURE THREE

ACCESS CONTROL

Perhaps no other countermeasure is more property specific than that of access control.

By definition, access control is that countermeasure which is utilized to monitor, control, influence, direct or restrict pedestrian and vehicular traffic onto, from and within a property.

From this definition it is patently obviously that every property's access control profile must be, by virtue of the total physical environment of that property, unique and individual.

In developing an access control survey checklist, a typical low-rise, medium-sized property is envisioned.   It is located in an urban setting and surrounded on its four sides by an open lot, an urban thoroughfare, a fenced commercial property and an alley separating it from another commercial property.   In such a setting, the survey/checklist might be concerned with the questions which follow. Obviously such a survey/checklist must be property-specific and must examine those issues which the individuality of the property presents.

Is there pedestrian or vehicular access from the perimeter by which an unauthorized person can utilize to gain un-monitored access to occupied buildings?

Are there appropriate warnings and prohibited-access signs posted?

Are such signs well maintained and written in appropriate languages?

Is there evidence of "attractive nuisances" which could invite unauthorized access, particularly to youths?

Are such "attractive nuisances" properly protected by individual barriers?

Are existing access control barriers at the property perimeter in good repair--fences, shrubs, culverts, etc.?

Are existing access barriers at the property perimeter effective as deterrents or do they in some cases provide a hiding place or de-facto invitation to unauthorized entry?

Are existing access barriers at the property perimeter affected by seasons or temperatures which might necessitate intermittent changes?

Are speed bumps appropriately placed and appropriately marked?

Are gates, both permanent and temporary, properly placed and maintained?

Have access control barriers, which were designed for a balanced combination of their aesthetics and access control, remained in that designated balance?

Has consideration been given to temporary placement of barriers to accommodate different traffic requirements at different times of the day?

If unauthorized and uncontrolled/undetected access is possible to certain outbuildings, are they, themselves secured against unauthorized entry?

Have valuable contents of vulnerable buildings been reduced or moved, when possible, to a more secure area?

Are such buildings periodically checked and monitored and is such checking documented?

Are appropriate restricted-entrance signs clearly and appropriately placed and maintained?

Is appropriate locking protection provided at access points of important buildings (particularly those which house guests or employees) which are not in constant view of an employee?

Is such locking protection monitored and checked at a regular and scheduled basis?

Is access control to such buildings determined by guest and asset protection or has guest/employee convenience been the driving determining factor?

Are employee entrances appropriately controlled, monitored and protected?

Is such monitoring documented and is the documentation retained?

Are such buildings equipped with appropriate limited access signs?

Are rooms/areas which require extensive access properly controlled?

Are rooms/areas which require limited access properly equipped with signs?

Is such locking monitored, controlled, verified, enforced and documented?

Is such documentation retained?

Is special access control attention given to storage and linen rooms which could be particularly hazardous?

Is access by elevator to restricted floors controlled with appropriate keys?

COUNTERMEASURE FOUR

LIGHTING

The countermeasure "lighting" falls into the expanded property-specific category into which access control fell.

It is again obvious that this countermeasure by its nature and by the vast difference between properties must be specifically individualized. The same typical low-rise property which was envisioned in the access control survey/checklist sample is used again in the lighting countermeasure example.

Does all lighting--interior, exterior, emergency--meet appropriate code?

How can this fact be documented?

Is there a written policy on property-wide lighting?

Does this policy address both lighting placement and coverage?

Does it require periodic inspections and preventive maintenance of all interior and exterior lighting?

(NOTE: A rule-of-thumb to measure lighting adequacy suggests that during the darkest hours, the surveyor should attempt to read a standard newspaper with existing light. If this can be accomplished, the area is likely to be adequately lit.)

Is this policy monitored, enforced and audited and are such audits maintained?

Is there a policy for and training provided whereby all employees should report lighting discrepancies?

Is both this policy and training monitored, enforced and audited and are these audits maintained?

When surveying or walking the property during darkened hours, does the absence of lighting cause fright or concern?

If so, are there areas where this is particularly true?

Is there a correlation between such threatening locations and areas which are commonly traveled by guests or employees?

If such areas exist, are there alternative countermeasures in place to counteract this, until or unless, the effected areas are addressed?

Are guest and employee parking areas adequately lit?

Are path and walk and driveways particularly well lit?

Are there shrubs or other potential hiding places which the lighting does not adequately cover?

If so, have companion countermeasures been employed?

Are access points to buildings particularly well lit?

Are interior guestroom building halls adequately lighted?

Does emergency lighting meet all appropriate code?

Is there a policy which requires the maintenance department to perform regular inspection and preventive maintenance on the emergency lighting?

Is this policy monitored, enforced and audited?

Are such audits maintained?

If protection officers are utilized on the property, are they required to note any lighting discrepancies on their logs?

Are such logs reviewed on a daily basis and are work orders immediately prepared and forwarded?

Does the maintenance department respond to these work orders in an expedient manner and are the timing and completeness of such actions documented and retained?

Is there a policy which requires the MOD to inspect lighting at least once a night?

Is this policy monitored, enforced and documented?

Is such documentation retained?

COUNTERMEASURE FIVE

KEY CONTROL

In preparing this sample survey checklist for the countermeasure key control, the same position has been taken which was discussed fully in chapter five.

Concentration has been placed on and limited to a survey/checklist of the guestroom.   The checklist has been developed using a hypothetical property which utilizes a mechanical keying system.

(NOTE: Obviously those properties which have the luxury of an electronic keycard system can and must develop a survey/checklist appropriate for such a system. Such a checklist normally is a fairly easy process utilizing the instructions and procedural tools provided by the maker of the electronic system adopted.)

Has a written key control policy been prepared and is it in use on the property?

Are protection considerations given to the following elements:

* Key production
* Key issuance
* Key retrieval
* Key inventory

THE E KEY

Is the number of E keys rigidly limited?

Have E keys been issued to only those persons/locations absolutely requiring them? (Have convenience and ego played any part of this issuance decision?)

Has E key production been stringently controlled, monitored and inventoried?

Is the storage of all issued E keys strictly controlled, monitored and inventoried?

Is every use of every E key recorded and justified?

Are records of and justification for the use of the E key monitored and retained?

Is the removal of an E key from the property prohibited and is this restriction monitored and enforced?

Are there provisions for scheduled audits of E keys and are such audits monitored, controlled and recorded?

Is a system in effect which allows for the rapid and effective response to a misplaced E key?

THE MASTER (AND SUB-MASTER KEYS)

Does the mastering key system allow for appropriate sub-mastering?

Is the issuance of master/sub-master keys strictly controlled?

Are such controls monitored, enforced, audited and records retained?

Is a strict sign in/sign out system maintained?

Are master keys securely attached to room attendants at all times?

Is this system monitored, enforced, audited and records retained?

If coding has been utilized, does such coding allow for ease of inventory, issuance and control?

Is a system in effect which would alert management if a key is missing or has left the property?

Is a system in effect to quickly and effectively react if a key is missing or has left the property?

Are audits of the keys conducted periodically and are the results of these audits retained?

GUESTROOM KEYS

Is a key par established at an appropriate level?

Does automatic recoring/re-keying/rotation occur at a specified time?

Is this system strictly monitored, enforced and audited?

Are these audits maintained?

Are key markings sufficiently disguised so as not to identify the guestroom number?

Is a system in effect at the front desk to eliminate the verbalizing of the guestroom number when issuing a key to a guest?

Is this system monitored, controlled and audited?

Are guestroom keys stored in a secured drawer or cabinet out of view and access to other than authorized persons?

Is front desk inventory of keys done on a daily basis?

Is such inventory monitored, controlled, enforced and are the audits retained?

Is a system in effect which limits the issuance of keys to identified guests only?

Is this system monitored, controlled, enforced and audited and are the audits retained?

Is a system in effect which provides appropriate protection when additional keys are requested?

Is a system in effect which directs front desk personnel to remind departing guests to turn in their keys?

Are room attendants equipped with locked key boxes on their carts?

Are such boxes emptied and the collected keys returned to inventory on a daily basis?

Are room attendants trained to deny access to guestrooms to anyone and to refer such requests to appropriate authority?

Are room attendants instructed on the correct procedure for key retrieval when keys are found in or around guestrooms?

Is this system monitored, controlled and enforced?

ALL KEYS

Is a system of key-production requests in effect which allows for close monitoring and control of reproduction orders?

Is this system monitored, controlled, enforced and audited?

Is the key-cutting machine stored in a secure location to which access is restricted and controlled?

Are key blanks controlled by a designated level of management?

Are key blanks and the key-cutting machine separated?

Is a multi-layered, work-order system in effect which allows a recoverable paper trail audit from the point of request to the point of delivery?

Is a system in effect which triggers immediate maintenance attention to sensitive key replacements?

Is a system in effect which assures that keys temporarily issued to bell or valet employees are property controlled?

Is a system in effect which teaches all employees the importance of key control and proper procedure when a protection matter involving keys occurs?

COUNTERMEASURE SIX

PROTECTION OFFICERS

When surveying the countermeasure Protection Officers, the General Manager can expect the necessity of nighttime and weekend survey activity.

> Does a specific protection criterion exist for the size and composition of the force?

> Who is responsible for selecting, hiring, training, supervising, disciplining and promoting protection officers?

> If these managerial functions are placed in the hands of outside contractors, is there a system of in-house verification that such functions are being accomplished?

> Does protection officer training include every proactive and reactive action desired by management?

> Is such training required upon employment and then intermittently throughout the career of that officer on the property?

> Is such training documented and the documentation retained for an appropriate amount of time?

> If contract officers are employed, has property management set down the contractual obligations?

> Are protection officers controlled, supervised and monitored to the same extent that other employees are?

> Are protection officers utilized at times and locations which maximize their proactive protective quality?

If protection officers are required to patrol, are their routes and the timing of those routes consistent with their proactive, protective quality?

If protection officers provide escort service, is such service effectively advertised to both guests and employees?

If protection officers provide inspection services, are such inspections double checked for compliance and accuracy?

If off-duty police are utilized as protection officers, have appropriate contractual agreements been executed with the appropriate police departments?

If weapons are carried by security officers, is this done with the knowledge and approval of hotel management, ownership, counsel and insurance carriers?

If weapons are carried by security officers, have approved and certified weapons training been conducted?

If weapons are carried by security officers, can such action be justified?

COUNTERMEASURE SEVEN

GUESTROOM PROTECTION

When surveying guestroom protection, the GM should concentrate not only at the guestroom locations themselves, but also at related departments.

GUESTROOM

Does the guestroom key work as designed?

Does the appropriate sub-master and E key work as designed?

Are there secondary security devices on the guestroom doors?

If so, are they in good working order?

Are self-closing guestroom door devices installed?

If so, are they in good working order?

Is there a self-locking feature on the guestroom door locking device?

If so, is it in good working order?

Are there viewing devices (peepholes) installed?

If so, are they installed at appropriate heights?

Is the State Innkeepers' Statutes displayed according to state requirements?

Is the guestroom directory in place and complete?

If so, is it in good repair and easily readable?

If so is it printed in several appropriate languages?

Are there appropriate and sufficient protection notifications in the guestroom?

Is there appropriate guidance which informs the guest of the nature of and his expected response to the sounding of audible alarms or the flashing of lights?

Are connecting doors secured from unauthorized entry from adjoining rooms?

Are windows secure as required by property procedures?

Is the telephone in proper working order?

Is there a "protection video channel" installed on the television?

If so, is it in good working order and appropriately complete?

Are fire warnings appropriately placed?

Are evacuation instructions and routes appropriately placed?

Are instructions for receiving rapid and appropriate assistance clearly posted?

If so, are such instructions posted in appropriately sufficient quantity?

FRONT DESK

Are the audible announcements of a guest's room ever made?

Is it possible for a phone caller to ascertain a guest's room number?

Is it possible for a person asking at the front desk to ascertain a guest's room number?

Is a rigid prearranged set of identifying procedure in place which prevents an unauthorized person from obtaining a key to a guestroom?

Is the issue of a second or subsequent key to a guest noted on the folio?

Are procedures in effect which signal when key par has been reached and which trigger appropriate actions?

BELL STAFF

Has the bell staff been scripted in dialogue and demonstrations which result in guests being informed of protection methods and devices?

Does the bell staff perform "de facto" mini-inspections of protective devices as such devices are being explained to the guest?

Is a method in place for the bell staff to report to maintenance or engineering irregularities observed in protection items in the guestroom?

HOUSEKEEPING STAFF

Are room attendants required to inspect and then note protection irregularities? This list might include:

*   Improperly operating locking devices
*   Improperly operating secondary locking devices
*   Improperly operating automatic door closing devices
*   Improperly operating telephones
*   Improper posting or poor condition of protection signs (e.g., alarm notifications, evacuation postings, Innkeeper laws, etc.)
*   Improper installation or adjustment of the viewing device?

Are room attendants required to note and properly safeguard found property?

Are room attendants required to note and appropriately report any suspicious activity in their work areas?

NOTE: If room attendant checklists are not employed by the property, are these items addressed in indoctrination and subsequent in-service training and is such training documented?

MAINTENANCE/ENGINEERING STAFF

Is there a system to flag work orders and require that they be expedited when such work orders have to do with protection items?

Does the work order system allow for an audit trail which will disclose time of receipt, source/method of reporting, time of dispatch and corrective action and time of completion?

Are completed work orders appropriately sequentially numbered, controlled, and maintained for an appropriate length of time.

Are safeguards in effect which allow only specified persons to authorize work orders?

Is there a system of maintenance/engineering guestroom inspections?

If so, are such inspections scheduled, performed as appropriate, and documented?

Are such inspections focused on the items which a room attendant or someone responsible for inspection might not recognize as a reportable item (e.g., structural damage?)

Are records of all guestroom-related governmental inspections maintained for an appropriate amount of time and corrective actions verified?

COUNTERMEASURE EIGHT

EMERGENCY RESPONSE

As indicated earlier, emergency response is the single reactive countermeasure as opposed to the seven other proactive countermeasures.

Regardless of this distinction, this countermeasure like all others must be personalized and developed with the specific property in mind. The reasons for personalization for this countermeasure are obvious: while some emergencies are virtually universal (fire is an example) many are property-specific. This is particularly true of emergencies surrounding weather.

As the survey/checklist is prepared, such property-specific emergency situations should be given appropriate consideration. The following is a generic survey/checklist from which an individualized one may be drawn.

Is there a written policy regarding the preparation for and the response to emergency response?

Has the policy been elevated to actual training?

If so, is such training conducted, monitored, enforced and documented?

Is there a system for monitoring, controlling, updating and enforcing this policy?

Is such documentation retained?

Have all appropriate emergencies been considered?

*   Severe weather (wind storms, snow conditions,
        flooding, severe temperatures)
*   Medical emergencies: Minor (first aid), Major (life-
        threatening), unusual (childbirth or on-property
        deaths)
*   Criminal (property crimes and person crimes)
*   Fire (prevention, detection, annunciation,
        suppression, evacuation)
*   Public demonstrations
*   Significant accidents (traffic accidents, chemical
        spills, aircraft accidents, etc.)

Are organized responses in effect for each of the emergency
possibilities and has training been given?

Has appropriate training been designed for each of these
emergency situations?

Is such training actually presented, monitored, enforced and
documented?

Is such documentation retained?

Is there written policy regarding the return of the property to
normal operations?

POINTS TO PONDER

PROTECTION MANAGEMENT SURVEY

◆   Discuss the importance of a property survey given that many GMs believe they are already thoroughly knowledgeable of all aspects of their property.

◆   Determine what level(s) of management should conduct the property survey and defend your position.

◆   Discuss how the results of a property survey should be used in three distinct settings.

◆   Explain why an initial property survey should be "diagnostic" rather than "remedial."

CHAPTER SEVEN

THE WAGON WHEEL AND THE PROTECTION MANAGEMENT COMMITTEE

Throughout this text, we have learned that the entire approach to guest protection is steeped in four separate phases:

I   Identifying and examining the assets which an Innkeeper must protect. (Our principal concern is the guest.)

II   Identifying and examining threats to which these assets are exposed. (Particularly crime.)

III   Developing countermeasures which minimize those threats.

IV   Integrating the resulting guest-protection profile into the entire property-management scheme.

We have seen also that the management model labeled the Protection Management Matrix can be used to illustrate those assets and threats isolated in phases I and II. Finally, we have seen that the eight identified countermeasures may be placed within that matrix to portray the protection afforded each asset from each threat.

What we have done, in effect, is to pull together the *ingredients* and place them on the table for the GM to utilize. What remains is for the GM to apply management-science techniques to these ingredients and make them work.

Recall, finally, our earlier emphasis on both responsibility and accountability. If the guest protection program is ever to come to total fruition and be effective, the GM must address those two concerns. This can be accomplished by the adoption of an organizational approach called the Protection Management Committee and the use of a management model entitled the Protection Management Wagon Wheel.

THE PROTECTION MANAGEMENT COMMITTEE

Most hoteliers have grown up in the lodging business accepting, utilizing and managing Safety Committees. Traditionally, these committees have addressed, as the name implies, the issue of "safety"--that discipline concerned with protecting employees from accidents and injuries. The committees have been composed of representatives from various departments and have traditionally met once or twice a month. The typical agenda concerned itself with such items as a torn carpet, the need for better snow removal, or a concern regarding slip-and-fall incidents in the housekeeping department.

Safety, again, traditionally in the mind of the hotelier, has dealt with a concern for protecting an identified asset (the employee) from an identified threat (accidents and injuries.) While this may be and indeed is necessary and effective, what this body has not addressed proactively are the other ingredients shown on our Protection Management Matrix. It would be unusual to find, for example, on a typical safety committee's agenda any of the following items:

> A concern about reports of the odor of alcohol on the breath of a newly-hired van driver.

> The non-English speaking room attendant who has not been instructed in techniques of limiting guestroom access to authorized guests.

The front desk clerk who has occasionally and casually given the E key to a maintenance person when a minor emergency occurred.

The security guard who seems to be consistently unavailable from 1 a.m. to 3 a.m.

Complaints from late shift dining room employees that the lighting in the employee parking lot has fallen into disrepair.

In short, it would be unusual to expect to see any agenda item outside the traditional scope of safety (i.e., a traditional worker's compensation concern.)

The adoption of the protection management committee model, however, changes the face and effectiveness of this body. The body already exists on most properties. It is a simple matter for the GM to rename it and give it new direction.

Imagine a charge to this newly-named committee which reads like the mission statement found on the following page. Initial resistance can almost certainly be expected--everyone resists change. The GM can and should respond to this challenge with management and leadership skills. He must address and educate the group as follows:

Educate them as a group that the courts **demand** reasonable care and that each of their jobs and their careers may depend on the property satisfying this requirements.

Educate them to the fact that while society has apparently been unsuccessful (or unwilling) to make crime prevention work, it can and must be addressed on their property.

Educate them to the fact that such crime prevention is not complicated, not expensive, not extremely labor intensive and its techniques can be learned and realized.

THE PROTECTION MANAGEMENT COMMITTEE

The Committee will be composed of representatives from every department on the property.

The Committee will be chaired by the General Manager   and have the responsibility for establishing and   maintaining an acceptable level of protection on the   property.

The Committee will address the following assets:

* The guests
* The employees
* The physical assets of the property

The Committee will address the following threats:

* fire
* accident/injuries
* natural disaster, and
* crime

The committee will function as an evaluative body, having oversight authority and the responsibility of assigning to it's own members certain protection tasks.

Educate them to the fact that there are eight countermeasures which, when adopted and applied, virtually assure success.

And educate them, finally, to the fact that not only is each of them qualified to take a major role in this task, all of them are going to be given the opportunity to do so.

Harken back to the organizational chart originally prepared by CHRIE and shown in chapter one. Recall that in that sample organizational chart seven manager-level employees are shown reporting directly to the GM.

* Director of personnel
* Sales manager
* Controller
* Food and Beverage manager
* Front Office manager
* Housekeeping manager
* Engineer

For the sake of discussion, let us assume that an eighth management-level position also is included, that being a security manager.

It is a reasonable assumption that the employees filling these eight positions should comprise the membership of the newly named protection management committee. (Additionally, the position of the GM is constant both on the organizational chart and as the head of that committee.)

Consider the impact of assigning management responsibility for these eight countermeasures individually to each of these eight participants!

How could such an approach be implemented and managed? A management model exists which addresses this question. It is called the Protection Management Wagon Wheel.

Figure 7 - 1 depicts the Protection Management Wagon Wheel--a model which portrays the eight countermeasures.   It also portrays the GM as being the hub around which these eight countermeasures revolve.

FIGURE: 7-1

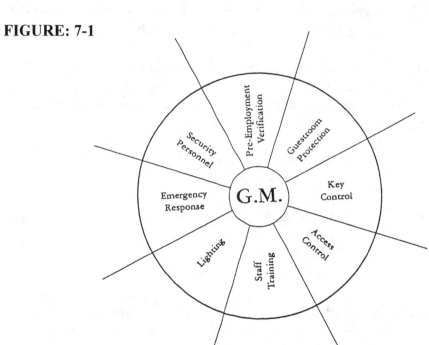

The concept of the Protection Management Committee married to the Wagon Wheel is realized when the GM identifies from his eight subordinate managers which manager will be responsible for which countermeasure.

For instance, the GM could assign the housekeeping manager to be responsible for the countermeasure Guestroom Protection.   The developing Wagon Wheel then would appear thus:

FIGURE: 7-2

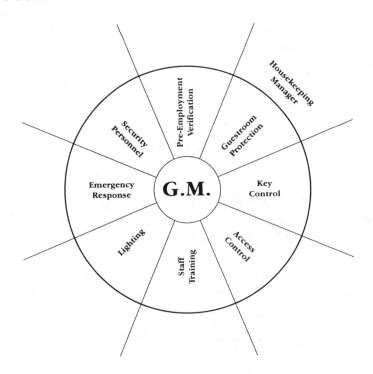

PROTECTION MANAGEMENT WAGONWHEEL

Figure 7-2 depicts the Protection Management Wagon Wheel with the inclusion of the selected manager adjacent to the countermeasure for which he is responsible.

If this concept were to be "sprung upon " the safety committee (now newly named the Protection Management Committee) what emotions could be expected--*particularly from the housekeeping manager*?

Fear?   Anger?   Denial?   Likely, yes, each and everyone of these.

Consider the following responses which could be expected following the decision to assign these new duties to the housekeeping manager.

"You mean you're actually going to force a functionary manager into an expanded decision-making position of accountability and responsibility?"

"What an outrageous idea!"

"To actually assign the responsibility of surveying and then maintaining a predetermined necessary level of protection within the guestroom--why, the housekeeping manager couldn't even learn that stuff!"

"Trust an employee who has, probably, only a high school education to actually be accountable for a major dimension of guest protection-- it just couldn't work!"

The GM's response to their negative objections should be crystal clear. Why should not the housekeeper be allowed to address a major management decision? Why indeed? The title Housekeeping Manager implies the <u>management</u> of the housekeeping department.

Why should the housekeeper **not** be given an enhanced level of responsibility? We have already seen an example of the GM who claims "everyone is responsible for security on my property." *Now let him back up that assertion by making a particular person responsible and accountable.*

Who on staff, for instance, knows more about the guestroom than the housekeeping manager? Who on staff, additionally, has a larger number of subordinates (room attendants) than the housekeeping manager?

The entire Protection Management Committee must likewise be educated. The GM can indeed educate them by addressing this entire new concept.

* He can address it by reminding all of them that they are already "managers." A "manager," he should remind them does not act simply as a functionary. (e.g., the housekeeping <u>manager</u> does not simply "run" the housekeeping department but manages it in its entirety.) Guest protection, then, within that department, is already the housekeeper's responsibility.

* He can address it by reemphasizing the value, the advantages and the absolute necessity of guest protection.

* He addresses it by assuring the group that he (the GM) has already surveyed each department and each countermeasure, and his survey will act as their roadmap. (See chapter six.)

* Finally the GM will emphasis to each manager that the particulars of the assigned countermeasures may be found in chapters seven though fifteen and that a compliance check list has been developed by the GM from the samples shown in chapter six.

Essentially, then, the GM is "leading."

* He has identified the challenge

* He has assigned responsibility

* He has provided working tools

* He expects accountability

The actual process begins when each particular manager accepts his particular countermeasure responsibility (along with the GM's diagnostic survey.) He then refers to the particular countermeasure chapter (chapter eight through fifteen) and learns the peculiarities of that particular countermeasure.

Acting within an assigned period of time, (a week perhaps, several weeks, maybe) the manager develops a working familiarity with the assigned countermeasure.

*   He develops an understanding of the threats against which his countermeasure can be effective

*   He determines what assets his countermeasure will protect.

*   He becomes familiar with the physical locations on the property where his countermeasures are currently applied and evaluates their effectiveness.

*   He determines where his countermeasure should be newly introduced.

These actions, repeated by each manager, will constitute the initial evaluative responsibility of the committee. To complete their evaluative responsibility, the committee will receive all eight individual diagnoses. Combining these reports with the initial property survey previously conducted by the GM, the committee will evaluate:

*   The type and criticality of threats which exist on the entire property. (See chapter four.)

*   The identity and peculiarities and "uniqueness" of their property's assets. (See chapter four.)

*   The identity, effectiveness and appropriateness of the existing countermeasures already in place. (See chapter four.)

*   In total, they will evaluate the entire protection profile of the property.

The full committee then has acted as an oversight group. They have addressed the subject countermeasures (each of them in turn) and collectively decided which are appropriate, necessary, effective, need adjustment or in need of being downgraded.

The committee reports to the GM its findings. The GM then considers the committee's recommendations, adjudicates, and assigns specific managers to be responsible for specific countermeasures.

Figure 7 - 3 on the following page depicts a sample completed Protection Management Wagon Wheel. And at this point, a discussion of these suggested assignments (some of which may be surprising) is appropriate.

Certainly a major consideration for selection should be each candidate-manager's strengths and capabilities. Another consideration should be steeped in the realization that management integration and counterbalance will strengthen the property management profile. This approach is illustrated below by the occasional avoidance of assigning to a manager the countermeasure with which he deals regularly. (We did not, for instance, assign PEV to the HR manager.)

Let's review the sample completed Protection Management Wagon Wheel assignment:

(1)   Guestroom protection: Already tentatively assigned to the housekeeping manager for the reasons shown earlier.

(2)   Access control: Why not the sales manager? This assignment not be as strange as it might appear at first glance. The sales manager is in the business of selling the property. Why not get him out of the office? Why not require that manager to learn the geography of the property by evaluating its access control?

FIGURE: 7-3

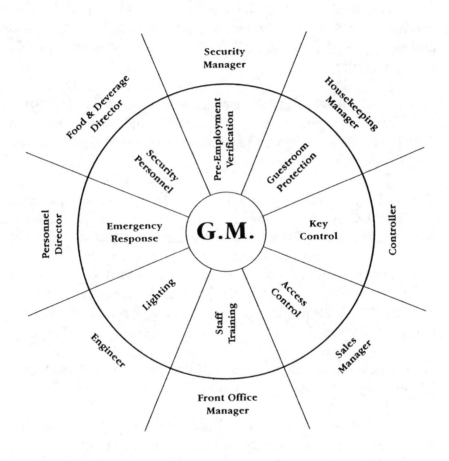

PROTECTION MANAGEMENT WAGONWHEEL

(3)   Key control: Is there rationale for assigning the controller to this countermeasure? There may be. We have suggested that inadequate key control has been historically the Achilles heel in civil litigation. Why not assign this countermeasure to the person responsible for controlling our money?

(4)   Staff training: Why suggest the front office manager for this assignment? The reason is apparent. Staff training is perhaps the broadest countermeasure of all and reaches out to every department. No department manager is more centrally located than the front office.

(5)   Lighting: The engineer is an obvious choice. He can affect inspection and maintenance schedules and ascertain that they are adhered to.   This assignment might has the advantage of assuring night-time inspections.

(6)   Emergency response: Assigning the personnel director to this broad discipline allows him more extensive exposure to the exposures property than he might otherwise have.

(7)   Pre-employment verification: There is rationale for not having assigned, as we might have been tempted, the director of personnel to this countermeasure. Understandably, HR-trained persons often tend to lean toward protecting a property by focusing on what it *cannot* do from a legal standpoint, rather than focusing on what it *must* do from a protection standpoint. Let's allow our security director (in concert with HR) to be in charge of pre-employment verification.

(8)   Security personnel: The obvious choice for this countermeasure normally would have been the security director. The security function, however, often can benefit from management outside its own disciple. Toward this end, let's allow the F&B manager to be responsible for this countermeasure and expand his managerial horizons.

POINTS TO PONDER

THE WAGON WHEEL AND THE PROTECTION MANAGEMENT COMMITTEE

◆   Identify the eight countermeasures which may be selected and employed to reduce the likelihood of crime occurring to a guest.

◆   Describe briefly, the value of each of the eight countermeasures.

◆   Select one of the countermeasure which you feel may be perhaps the single most effective one and defend your position.

◆   Discuss the concept of the Protection Management Wagon Wheel.

◆   Discuss, from a protection management standpoint, reasons that the adoption of the protection management wagon wheel may be advantageous.

◆   Discuss what you consider to be an ideal manning composition of a Protection Management Committee.

◆   Describe how a Protection Management Committee differs from the traditional lodging concept of a Safety Committee.

EXECUTIVE SUMMARY OF PART THREE

HOTEL PROTECTION MANAGEMENT

Part three presents a concentrated view of each of the eight countermeasures.

It is important to remember that there are, generally, no established and specific "security" standards within the lodging industry. As stressed throughout this text, each property is unique unto itself--each has different threats and different assets. It follows, then, that as a property protection program is being developed (or adjusted) that the selected countermeasures should be appropriate to protect those unique assets against the unique threats.

The countermeasures are not necessarily arranged and presented in order of their importance. Rather they are shown in a logical sequence with the aim that the "bad guys" (e.g., the threat of crime) are to be kept away from the guest (the number one asset.) Imagine the route which the bad guys can be expected to take. Consider how that sequence is arranged to intercept the threat and protect the guest.

(1)   Pre-employment verification (PEV): Recall that a high percentage of crime involves and sometimes is caused by the employee. It is logical, therefore, to begin guest protection with a countermeasure designed to keep a potential criminal from ever *becoming* an employee. Pre-employment verification is the principal countermeasure designed to accomplish that protection.

(2)   Staff training: Once the applicant has succeeded in passing the PEV hurdle he obviously becomes an employee. Staff training, the second countermeasure, is designed to

provide to that employee the tools he needs to become an active player in the guest protection scheme.

(3)   Access Control: Once PEV and training have secured the guest from *internal* threats, it is time to concentrate on the perimeter of the property and attempt to thwart the *external* threat. This third countermeasure, addresses that concern by attempting to control access at specified points.

(4)   Lighting: Should the external "bad guy" circumvent the access control barriers, the next line of defense against him is lighting. Simply stated, if he gets past the perimeter of the property (or any other controlled point) lighting, it is hoped, will either deter or reveal him.

(5)   Key control: The next countermeasure designed to reduce the commission of crime is key control. As the hypothetical criminal moves ever closer to the guest, the successful installation and maintenance of a key control system is the next effort designed to deter him.

(6)   Protection officers: Protection officers, utilized either at fixed posts or in roving assignments can detect and intercept this threat as it moves toward the guest.

(7)   Guestroom protection: The guest is most vulnerable while in his guestroom. The final "line of defense" then, is at this point. Guestroom protection should be a combination of effective and well-conceived techniques and tools designed to provide the guest with an effective barrier.

(8)   Emergency response: Should the seven proactive countermeasures above fail to deter the threat of crime, emergency response, a reactive countermeasure, comes into play. The staff should be trained to react quickly and effectively when any emergency occurs.

CHAPTER EIGHT

PRE-EMPLOYMENT VERIFICATION

"EMPLOYMENT" according to David Gyongyos, a noted hospitality human resource consultant in Scottsdale, Arizona, "is not an *act,* it is a *process.* "

This position bears examination, discussion, and amplification.

Dr. Gyongyos explains that employment, as a process, entails all the aspects of that most useful tool available to the lodging manager-- MANPOWER (recall this M tool from our management clown figures.)

Employment, as a process, may begin with the search for an employee to fill a vacant or newly created position. The *employment process* may continue when applicants begin appearing in response to an advertisement or notice of vacancy.

That process continues again when applicants formally apply, are considered, rejected, interviewed, tested, and hired. It does not end here, however, according to Gyongyos.

The *employment process* continues throughout the life of the employment, from initial job placement, to training, to motivation, to supervision, to discipline and to promotion.

It extends literally to all aspects of the persons working life from the moment he views the announcement of a vacancy until he leaves the organization. *E*mployment is a continuum which ranges on and on for any given employee. It is indeed more than a *single act.*

Therefore, when corporations proclaim that "people are our most important resource" they are not simply voicing PR gibberish. People, indeed, are the most important tool a manager has. Without them, he is totally dependent--until or unless total automation replaces us all.

Employees, in some ways, may be likened to the guest. We have seen that without the guest (our number one asset) the property simply cannot survive. So also without the employee the manager simply cannot function.

Obviously given these facts, no small amount of planning, effort and attention must be given to the process of employment. Early in that process must be the considerations for *pre-employment verification.*

Pre-employment verification, of the eight countermeasures available to a manager, is considered by many experts to be the *paramount* one available--particularly against crime. Why should this be so? The answer is at the same time rather simple and rather astounding.

Consider the entire array of crimes which might befall a guest: armed robbery, room theft, criminal assault, battery, to name only a few. In virtually every case, *proximity to the guest-victim is a necessary ingredient. And who has more close proximity than the employee?* While this question may seem cold-hearted and disloyal, it is a consideration with which all Innkeepers must deal.

Innkeepers must accept the fact that while employees are the most vital of all *assets*, they also constitute an often unrecognized *threat* on the protection management matrix.

Consider the following:

> Who, more than any other, possesses the most *opportunity* to commit crime against the guest? The employee.

Who, more than any other, is in the proximity of the guest? The employee.

Who, more than any other, has the ability to access the guestroom? The employee.

No one, literally no one, is in a better position to perform a criminal act upon a guest or a guest's possessions than the employee.

Accepting these possibilities as fact, it is apparent that great care must be taken in the process of employment. The Innkeeper must be totally satisfied that the person finally selected for employment is the one most qualified, the one most appropriate, the one most suited, and above all the one most trustworthy. The Innkeeper, in other words, must "do" proper, extensive and systematic *pre-employment verification.*

When our nation was predominantly rural with the majority of the population located in small towns and communities, the task of selecting the best qualified applicant was relatively easy.

Everyone knew everyone else. One had but to mentally go down a list of possible applicants and review their past history.

*   Had their school attendance been favorable?

*   Had there been trouble with law enforcement?

*   Were they known in their neighborhood to be disruptive?

*   Were they active in church, athletics, or school activities?

The answers to any or all of these questions could come into play during a prospective employer's search for an applicant. This opportunity to mentally pre-screen applicants, for the most part, is no longer an employer's luxury.

Today, the prospective employer is faced with a myriad of difficult decisions when the prospect of employing a person must be faced.

When properly accomplished, however, these early steps in the employment process allow for an eventual workforce which can be superlative. *Failure*, however, to effectively "do" pre-employment verification can result in untold difficulties ranging from needless lost time and effort to adverse effects on the bottom line, to and including tragic results.

Consider a case in Arizona in which pre-employment verification was *not* properly conducted.

> On a given morning, a woman guest returned to her motel room after having had breakfast with her husband and seeing him off to his appointment at a nearby nuclear energy facility. Upon entering her room, she encountered an intruder. The intruder, panicked at being discovered, drew a knife and attacked the guest, killing her with multiple stab wounds.
>
> Following discovery of the body, it did not take local police long to locate and apprehend the assailant who was arrested, tried and convicted of murder.
>
> *The assailant turned out to be an employee of the property.*

The young man from a community several miles from the property had been hired to do general cleanup work. On the morning of the crime, he apparently saw the opportunity to gain access to the victim's room and did so. He was rifling the bureau when the guest returned to her room and surprised him.

He apparently acted on impulse. The criminal trial was quick and decisive and his conviction for murder was almost certain. The *civil* proceedings were next, and during this portion of the story, *it was the property itself which was put on trial.*

The family of the victim--the plaintiffs, in this case--brought civil suit against the property claiming it had been negligent in the hiring of the young man. They presented the jury the following arguments:

> The property owed to their client's relative--the murdered guest--a duty of care. You will recall that we have seen earlier in the text that the courts have held that care must be provided--reasonable care.

> They further contended that the property had failed to provide this duty of care by failing to screen properly their employees, specifically the one who eventually committed the murder. Finally they contended that it was that particular failure--the improper pre-employment verification procedures--had been the cause of death.

> The plaintiffs implored the jury to award compensatory damages (meaning monies to compensate for the loss of the victim, the related expenses and recompense for pain and suffering.)

> Additionally, plaintiffs asked to receive *punitive* damages. Punitive damages are those damages which may be sought and which may be awarded separately from and in addition to compensatory damages, as a means of punishing the offending party for negligence. Punitive damages are also designed to send a message to the public that circumstances such as the ones discussed in this Arizona case are not acceptable. Such damages often are extremely severe. In many states they *are not covered by liability insurance which*

> *means, obviously, that punitive awards come out of the bottom line of the property.*

In the Arizona motel case, plaintiff's attorney, during the process of discovery, requested and received the employment application originally filled out by the young man.

Examination of that employment application disclosed several items which plaintiff's attorneys used in their case. One of particular interest was the block on the form which requested a personal reference. The applicant had listed a neighbor.

When investigators for plaintiff interviewed the neighbor who had been shown as a reference, they discovered damning evidence which they later brought to the court and which was instrumental and pivotal in the jury's decision.

Under oath, the neighbor was asked if she was acquainted with the accused and she testified that indeed she was.

When asked about his background she testified that the accused had been a problem in the neighborhood for years, was untrustworthy and a threat. When asked, since she had been listed as a reference on the application form, why she had not informed the motel management about her concerns, she replied, "They never asked."

Plaintiff's attorney then was able to make the point to a sympathetic jury that this property was not willing to invest a twenty five cent phone call to verify the reliability of a prospective employee--twenty five cents for this woman's life.

The damages, both compensatory and punitive, amounted to several millions of dollars.

The motel no longer exists.

The family continues to grieve.

Plaintiff's attorney has been able to retire.

The case, while exceedingly illustrative, is not unique. There are cases of:

Convicted murders being discovered on the payroll of hotels.

Convicted child-molesters being employed as bellpersons.

Convicted embezzlers being in charge of accounting functions.

Convicted drunk-drivers being employed as van drivers.

Properties *needlessly* put their guests, other employees and in fact the very future of their businesses in jeopardy by failing to perform properly, consistently and systematically pre-employment verification.

While there may be explanations for such shortcomings, there are no excuses.

The act of pre-employment verification is crucial, vital and necessary. It is not difficult to perform and yet it is often poorly performed or not performed at all. Such performance places a property in great danger.

EMPLOYMENT -- THE PROCESS

It is critical to note that the employment process, in its entirety, must conform to all laws and regulations. There are federal, state and local requirements which must be understood and complied with--and different requirements exist in different locations.

Innkeepers must become knowledgeable about the laws which affect them in their particular locale. To do otherwise invites great difficulty and possible sanction

And these laws are changing virtually on a daily basis. Innkeepers must not only know and abide by these laws but keep continually aware of them and their changing status.

It is equally critical to note that consideration of the employment process-- particularly the pre-employment verification portion--is not something that is normally considered as being part of guest protection and reasonable care. **In fact, it is.**

One need go no further than the Arizona case discussed above to realize that guest protection begins long before the guest arrives at the property. One major part of that protection begins with the property's employment process, particularly pre-employment verification.

While this function may be and often is centered in the human resources department, it is indeed a property-wide consideration.

Perhaps nothing is more important to the protection of the guest than the reliability of the employee--a consideration which begins with pre-employment verification.

THE EMPLOYMENT APPLICATION FORM

In the case of the Arizona murder, plaintiff's attorneys found many clues to the crime in the original job application form.

Not only was the damning evidence there regarding the personal reference, they also discovered blanks and errors and even statements which might have been shown to be outright falsehoods.

This tragic case is an excellent example of how the application form, if it had been processed properly, (the twenty five-cent phone call) could have averted the terrible consequences.

Application forms are as varied in form and design as properties differ one from the other. They are alike, however, in that they often are the first clue that the hiring authority has in determining the qualifications of an applicant.

* Does he have the desired experience?

* Does he have the desired education?

* Does he have the desired traits?

* Does he have the desired abilities?

While the form should be designed to elicit sufficient information to assist in the selection process, it should only include *only those questions which are pertinent to the job in question.*

Subjects to be avoided include inquiries regarding national origins, race, color, political affiliations, religion, sex, marital status, economic status, and number of children.

The components of the application form may vary somewhat but certain basic information is called for on virtually all of them. This includes:

Applicant's personal data section: Full name, current address, telephone number and social security number.

Background data section: Pertinent job-related personal background data which includes both education and experience.

References section: Names of persons who can attest to his abilities, character, education and reliability.

Disclaimers section: In this section, normally in bold and clearly stated fashion immediately above the signature block, the applicant is informed of drug testing policy and policy of the property to engage in background verification including earlier employment criminal background and personal references. It should be stated that the property may use any or all job-related verification techniques which the property manager plans to utilize.

AGAIN, LEGAL COUNSEL SHOULD REVIEW AND APPROVE ANY OR ALL DISCLAIMERS PRIOR TO THEIR USE.

Accuracy verification and information release authorization section: In this section, typical application forms include statements regarding acknowledgment of the applicant that the information supplied is complete and accurate to the best of his knowledge. Any deliberate falsifications, misrepresentations or omissions may be grounds for not hiring or for subsequent dismissal if hiring has taken place. This is normally followed by a request that the applicant authorize the property to verify all information.

THIS ACCURACY VERIFICATION AND REFERENCE AUTHORIZATION ALSO MUST BE APPROVED BY LEGAL COUNSEL PRIOR TO USE.

PROCESSING THE APPLICATION FORM

The application form begins, not surprisingly (but often overlooked) with a review of the application form itself.

Total form completeness   Has the applicant completed every required blank and answered every required question? If not, the Innkeeper may wish to go no further but rather return it to the applicant for completion.

Example: Many application forms (with the approval of legal counsel) ask the question: "Have you ever been convicted of a felony?" Applicants may choose to ignore this question, often out of fear that disclosing such a history will disqualify them from consideration but fearful also of lying on the application. They decide instead simply to leave that question unanswered.

Specific question completeness   Has the applicant addressed the totality of each question to the satisfaction of the hiring authority?

Example: In the space requesting earlier employment job duties an applicant might indicate "supervised staff." This minimum response does not allow an ample amount of information from which to form even a preliminary hiring decision. The hiring authority needs to know, for instance, how many persons constitute "staff" what the applicant's duties as "supervisor" were; the extent of his authority, etc.

Continuity   Has the applicant provided continuity of activity, for instance, in the section detailing earlier employment? Is there an unbroken time line or are there gaps which are unexplained? Often this may be an oversight and can be easily explained. Sometimes such gaps in the time line may be purposeful.

Example: Applicants who have periods of their life which they feel will be disqualifying in nature simply skip that time frame and go on to the next. If an applicant had a period of employment from which he was dismissed for cause, he may feel that disclosing such a time or such background will preclude his hiring.

Clarity   If the position in question requires a degree of clear, concise writing skills, has the applicant shown such skills on the application form?

Example: If the applicant is, for instance, applying for a protection officer position and the duties of that position require on-the-spot, clear and concise report writing, are such skills exhibited on the application form?

THE INTERVIEW

In the employment process, the interview should be conducted following processing the application form and immediately before the extensive pre-employment verification process.

While the employment process is often centered in the Human Resources department, and preliminary steps conducted there, interviews by the person to whom the applicant will report directly are vital.

In many cases, such supervisors may not have had the opportunity to learn and practice effective interview techniques. Such techniques need to be learned simply because if they are members of the management team then a part of management is the supervising of employees.

During the interview   It is during this time that the interviewer has unequaled opportunity to observe the applicant first hand and view and listen and almost have a   sense of what the applicant is about.

He can determine certain behavioral patterns such as communication ability, personal grooming standards, ability to listen and apparent ability to understand, alertness, and ability to be at ease.

The application form can establish the basis for the formal part of the interview process. The interviewer can, and should, go over each item of the form individually, verifying the applicant's understanding of the query and the completeness of the response.

Particular attention should be given to the extent of the applicant's fitness for the job in question--his skills, experience, education and attitude.

Related applicant characteristics may also be addressed such as interests, hobbies, and ambitions.

The particulars of the job should be previewed. Discuss what the applicant will be expected to do, the hours involved, the tasks, and the environment. Only by a realistic and honest discussion of these factors can an applicant be expected to determine if he is interested (irrespective of any interest the supervisor may have regarding him.)

Interviewers must be taught that the subjects to be avoided on the application form must also be avoided during the interview.

The next step . . . PRE EMPLOYMENT VERIFICATION

To this point in the chapter, we have seen that great care must be taken in the early stages of the employment process. From the design and style of the job application form, to the processing of that form, to the interview process--all have been preludes to the possible decision to hire. One major step remains, and that step is the crux of this chapter.

It is called Pre-Employment Verification. (PEV)

PEV is an integral and vital part of the employment process, one which can be of tremendous benefit to an employer. When overlooked, it can be tragic. So what exactly does pre-employment verification entail and what is its value?

There are lodging managers who feel apprehension about not only "doing PEV" but about the subject itself in our world of host-related endeavors. Doing a "background check" on a prospective employee seems to some as bad if not worse than the taboos surrounding our old word "security." Not only is this position not defendable, it is counterproductive.

When done correctly, there is nothing unethical, unlawful, or immoral about PEV. On the contrary, failure to accomplish such a vital employment process task can be dangerous and subject a property to great perils.

NOTE: Again, care must be taken to stay within the bounds of legality while accomplishing this necessary function. At the end of this chapter there is advice on how to avoid such problems by verifying, state by state, what laws affect this process and how to comply.

There are other lodging managers who, as an excuse not to accomplish PEV, claim that the necessity of hiring an application *immediately* (typically to satisfy a function that very night) prohibits pre-employment verification. While the need to hire in an emergency is a dilemma, the answer to the dilemma is obvious. When time constraints demand immediate hiring, then it should be done. Immediately thereafter (while the new employee is into days or even hours of the probation period) the pre-employment process should begin. To do otherwise can be a serious and tragic mistake.

Failure to perform properly pre-employment verification prior to hiring or in the case cited above failing to accomplish it as soon as possible sets the scene for:

> Civil suits alleging failure to screen properly employees (when such lack of screening leads to an alleged crime against a guest)

A work force which is burdened with morale problems, knowing there are co-workers who should have been screened out prior to being employed

Higher than normal turnover in employment.

Low productivity brought on by a less than adequate work force.

Pre-employment verification is a win-win-win situation. Lack of it can be lose-lose-lose. Not only does it help a prospective employer to validate job experience, education and qualification, it has a myriad of other advantages.

A check of an applicant's criminal history, consistent with the law, may disclose convictions of a type which may cause further inquiry.

Example: A review of an applicant's criminal record might disclose a conviction for forgery some years back and a subsequent sentence which was carried out. Such a record might not be a major consideration if the applicant was applying, for instance, for a chef's position. On the other hand, if the applicant was applying for a position of lifeguard, then multiple convictions for the crime of child molestation would certainly be of interest to the prospective employer!

Motor vehicle department (MVD) records checking often provides a wealth of information.

Example: A review of MVD records in many states provides the correct spelling of the name, address, date of birth, and social security number of the applicant. Such data may be cross checked against the job application form to verify completeness and accuracy. Additionally, if the MVD review were to reveal multiple violations of local motor vehicle ordinances, then an applicant's desire to be the van driver might be questioned.

Workman's compensation records are often helpful.

Example: A review of workers' compensation records might reveal a disqualifying disability about which the hiring official was unaware and which might disqualify the applicant for a particular job.

Reference checks with persons having personal knowledge of the applicant can be revealing.

Example: A humorous but true example of a reference check revealing unexpected results was once experienced during a pre-employment exercise in a southwestern state. The hiring official called the *mother* of an applicant since the applicant had listed her as a reference. The position in question was one of bartender and the hiring official asked the reference (the mother) if she thought her son would make a good bartender. She replied "Yes, indeed he would and it sure would be nice to see him on that side of the bar for a change."

A review of vital statistics records can be of assistance.

Example: Vital statistics, like drivers records, can be a great help in verifying much of the information on the job application form (and remember this entire process is known as pre-employment verification.)

It is not simply an exercise which replaces the other aspects of the employment process. It is a verification that the other portions are valid.

METHODS UTILIZED IN THE PRE-EMPLOYMENT VERIFICATION PROCESS

There are several methods which may be utilized by an employer in the pre-employment verification process. They include face-to-face interviews, telephone checks, mail correspondence and the use of commercial firms which specialize in such verification. There are advantages to each.

Face-to-face verification   This method of PEV is often difficult or impracticable to perform. Particularly when the job opening is one which is relatively low on the pay scale and other methods of PEV are possible, this technique usually is not used.

If, however, the applicant is applying for a higher level position or if references are available from within the existing work force, this method is often valuable.

> Example: If an applicant is known to have an acquaintance on the payroll, inviting those acquaintances to be a reference can be invaluable.

Telephone verification checks This is the most commonly used method of PEV. The calls are usually quick and inexpensive. They are also less reliable than other methods. Many properties use a standardized check list which the caller uses as a reminder to cover all needed and desired subjects.

> Example: A prepared questionnaire, readily available to the person responsible for telephone checks, might list the following items:
>
> > Verification of employment
> > Verification of years of employment
> > Verification of unbroken work history
> > Verification of skills, education and training
> > Verification of punctuality, cooperation and reliability

These and other questions tend to multiply themselves. Once a caller, with tact and reason, persuades the earlier employer to cooperate, great amounts of information may be gleaned.

Mail verification   Use of the mails to accomplish PEV is inexpensive and can be useful. It is however quite slow. It is most useful when the information sought is lengthy and statistical in nature and not particularly time-sensitive or subject to interpretation.

Background verification firms   In virtually every city a review of the yellow pages will reveal firms who specialize in PEV. These firms, often listed under "employment or employee screening" will, for a fee, perform the function of pre-employment verification.

Of further assistance, National Employment Screening Services publishes a source directory for employee screening. *The Guide to Background Investigation* presents state-by-state brief summaries of what laws apply in each state regarding PEV. Included in this directory in addition to the brief discussion of what is and what is not allowed in each state is information such as:

Advice on how to obtain criminal records.

Restrictions on the use of polygraphs.

Limitations on inquiries about arrests not leading to convictions.

Addresses of courthouses from which PEV data may be obtained.

State "hotline" telephone numbers.

Methods by which driving records may be obtained.

How to obtain college records.

This document may be obtained by writing to National Employment Screening Services, 8801 South Yale Avenue, Tulsa, Oklahoma, 74137. (800) 247-8713 or (918) 491-9936. It sells, as of the publication of this text, for $124.94 plus S&H.

Another useful publication available from the same source is the *Social Security Number Guide* which explains how an employer can determine if a social security number has been falsified.

The thrust here is not to recommend any firm or one method or one approach over another. Rather it is to advise that these are methods and sources which may be used in the accomplishment of PEV. There is little justification for not doing PEV because "I didn't know how to get it done." Whatever the methods, ascertain that the HR representative or whomever else is responsible, maintains an appropriate record that the verification was done.

In court it is one thing to try and assure a jury that indeed an applicant *was* verified prior to employment. It is easier and more effective to be able to produce specific records to that effect.

<u>Make a record that the verification was done.</u>

POINTS TO PONDER

PRE-EMPLOYMENT VERIFICATION

◆ Define pre-employment verification as a countermeasure.

◆ Explain which step within the pre-employment process (the application, form, the interview and the actual verification) should be reviewed and approved by counsel.

◆ Explain the position that employment is a "process" more than a single act.

◆ Defend the position held by many hoteliers that the pre-employment verification is the paramount countermeasure available.

◆ Identify reasons why pre-employment verification is not utilized as thoroughly as it might be, given its reputation of extreme importance.

◆ Discuss why employment application forms play such an important role in the pre-employment countermeasure.

◆ Identify and discuss subjects to be avoided on the employment application form.

◆ Identify five traits which should be explored during the job application interview.

◆ Identify and discuss subject to be avoided during the job application interviews.

◆ Discuss possible problems which could arise if pre-employment verification we not accomplished effectively.

◆   Discuss the possible advantages of reviewing, during the pre-employment verification process, the applicant's history insofar as the following are concerned:

* Criminal history
* Motor vehicle records
* Workman's compensation records
* Reference checks
* Vital statistics

CHAPTER NINE

GUEST PROTECTION TRAINING

There is little doubt that training is vital to success in business, including of course the lodging business.

This statement is so patently obvious that there is a tendency to accept it without thought and yet because it is so obvious and valid, it bears comment and examination.

No business can hope to succeed without trained employees.

Manufacturing firms are virtually assured of failure without trained employees. Retail establishments have failed because they did not have trained employees. Public utilities, financial institutions, health care organization--all, without exception, are highly likely to fail unless the personnel responsible for the product or the service which is intended to be delivered to the public are trained.

In many service industries, including the lodging industry, a significant number of employees apply and are employed with little or no previous formal education or training. Even those who arrive with some degree of basic skills are not knowledgeable or informed of the particulars and peculiarities of their new property environment.

They require training.

No F&B manager would allow a chef to serve his customers without adequate training. No sales manager would allow a sales representative to call on a prospective account without adequate training. No front office manager would allow a front desk clerk to register a guest without adequate training.

<u>And no general manager should allow his guests to be placed at risk by not having his entire staff trained in guest protection</u>.

In civil court, time and again, properties have been held liable and suffered great financial loss, because of the failure to provide guest protection.

Room attendants have allowed unauthorized persons into rooms and thefts have occurred. Why? Because that room attendant had not been properly trained in guest protection.

Telephone operators have disclosed information about a guest which has resulted in assaults. Why? Because that operator had not been properly trained in guest protection.

Front desk clerks have provided keys to persons who claimed to be guests but were not. Tragedy results. Why? Because those front desk clerks had not been properly trained in guest protection..

In chapter eight we learned that employment is not an act, but rather a continuing process. So too, is training. At best, training in guest protection has been neglected and overlooked. At worst, it has been ignored. It must be emphasized.

TRAINING IN GUEST PROTECTION AND REASONABLE CARE

The process of training, that continuum which begins at the time the employee begins his employment and continues until he leaves that employment is crucial to the success of the property.

In literally every department, every manager must accept that fact.

Property success will not evolve unless and until every employee in every department is afforded the process of training in guest protection. Such training is vital because the lodging industry has a high turnover rate. Such training is vital because the lodging industry employs such a high rate of previously untrained persons. Such training is vital because the lodging industry is experiencing, not unlike many other industries, rapid technological changes. And most important such training is vital because protecting the guest must be the Innkeeper's prime concern.

Simply stated, this process--this continuum of training--is designed to accomplish three objectives:

(1)   teach employees how to perform new and unfamiliar tasks.

(2)   assist employees in improving current skills.

(3)   assure that the guest will be protected.

This chapter will examine elements of training programs which are particularly useful and necessary to the lodging industry as well as discuss various types of guest protection training methods which have proven effective over long term use.

Obviously the highest level of management on a property has overall training responsibility. In most individual properties, this means the GM. Often he assigns the responsibility to the human resource department, a unit usually well situated to oversee the plan.

The actual conduct of training, however, is often a vastly different concern and thus requires a vastly different approach. We will examine that approach in detail later in this chapter.

The initial consideration of guest protection training is that of determining needs--the preparing of a statement of training objectives. Such a statement allows for a common beginning point for all levels of employment from the prospective of management as well as the work force.

A sample guest protection training objective might read:

"This property is absolutely committed to the care and safety of its guests. Toward that commitment, every employee at every level in every department will receive sufficient detailed and documented training in the methods and safeguards of guest protection as is required.

"Such training will be accomplished at the time of hire, at the time of promotion or transfer, and on an ongoing basis during the employee's entire tenure with the property.

"Responsibility for guest protection training will rest with the human resources director who, in coordination with the protection management committee, will ascertain that specific tasking is assigned to each department as appropriate, validate that the training is accomplished and maintain training records.

"Although initial entry guest protection training may be a part of the overall new hire indoctrination program, specific in-service guest protection training will be accomplished departmentally.

"The entire scope of guest protection training will be reviewed at a minimum during every quality assurance review."

From this statement benchmark, then, the program can evolve.

INITIAL GUEST PROTECTION TRAINING NEEDS SURVEY

Training needs must initially be determined. This can be accomplished in several ways.

Determine the guest's wants and concerns. There is no surer method of determining guest protection training needs than actually listening to the guest himself. By reading complaint cards, by having the staff listen and report comments received from guests and by successfully utilizing guest comment cards, a significant amount of information may be gained.

NOTE: On one hand, a comment from a guest about his security can be extremely beneficial in isolating a training need. On the other hand, ignoring such a comment or failing to address it can be disastrous.

Determining what the line employees see as guest protection (and incidentally, their own personal protection needs) can be useful. Employees are usually the best source of information. They should be given not only the opportunity to voice their concerns, they should be urged to do so. If an employee sees a guest protection problem, then likely there has been a breakdown in the guest protection training program.

Determine what the supervisory staff views as actual or potential guest dangers or problems. Usually by soliciting this assistance, department by department, the best results ensue.

Finally, and perhaps most vital, the GM, during his periodic assessments of the property, should concentrate on those observable items which suggest changes or additions which are needed in the guest protection training program.

There are several methods in gleaning this data from several sources. Specifically, the conduit to and through the protection management committee should be fully utilized. Input from all levels of employees, input from guests, and input from vendors and contractors should filter through this committee. Appropriate corrective action then can be accomplished.

Individual interviews (e.g., during an evaluating session) are also used. This method is often valuable but it is time consuming and expensive when compared to others. Group interviews (e.g., during a departmental staff meeting) allow opportunity in an open atmosphere for employees to make their views known. Questionnaires are used quite frequently. Examples of questionnaires include guest comment cards and guest complaints. Guest protection consultants (usually calling themselves security consultants) can be valuable tools for determining guest protection training needs.

METHODS , ORGANIZATION, AND IMPLEMENTATION OF THE GUEST PROTECTION TRAINING PROGRAM

Organization and implementation constitute the second step in the development of the guest protection training program. It involves decisions regarding who will be trained, by whom, where and with what frequency.

The training population It should be a matter of policy that *all* employees, in all departments and at *all* levels will be trained in the specifics of guest protection. This policy should require that guest protection training be mandatory upon initial employment, upon transfer or promotion and on a scheduled basis throughout the career of the employee.

The trainers While the overall responsibility for training often lies within the human resource department, specific guest protection training is often best done within individual departments.   One reason for this is that the department head (and sometimes subordinate supervisors) is best equiped to manage training time and schedules.   Another reason is because guest protection training should be departmentally "threat-specific." That is to say, those threats which exist in one department may not exist in another and departmental concentration, therefore, for this training is usually advantageous.   Still another reason is that the personalities, capabilities, and needs of individual employees are best known to management personnel in their individual departments. Departmental training concentration therefore allows for attention to be given where need is most required.

Training methods   Training methods fall, generally, into two categories: group training and individual training.   Both have advantages and disadvantages but both should be considered, not only individually but in concert with one another when planning a guest protection training program.

GROUP TRAINING METHODS

Lecture approach   This includes any methods in which presentations before an assembled group are delivered. Normally, the group simply listens to lectures (not unlike college or university class).   The lecturer may supplement his presentation with visual aids and often concludes with questions, answers and discussions.

> Useful examples: This method is often used for guest
> protection indoctrination training to new property employees.
> Normally, an agenda is set and several managers or
> departments make prepared presentations. *This is the ideal
> time to introduce the property policy which stresses the
> absolute requirement that guests be protected at all times in
> all departments.*

Role-playing approach   This includes any of several approaches in which a scenario or circumstance is presented to the group and then roles are assigned or taken in order to demonstrate predetermined conclusions.   Individuals in the group act, intermittently, as participants and observers and as observers provide feedback to those playing the participative roles.

> Useful examples: This approach is particularly effective
> when a trainer has a specific circumstance or setting to be
> explored.   For instance: In a group meeting within the

housekeeping department, the executive housekeeper may decide to concentrate on the training of unauthorized access to a guestroom.

The housekeeper may assign one employee from the group the role of the room attendant working in the guestroom hallway and assign to another employee the role of an unknown person who is also found in that hallway. The unknown person can be invited to think of all the reasons he needs to get into a room ("I've locked my self out," or "I've left my briefcase inside") The employee playing the role of the room attendant must conjure up appropriate responses to each of the questions.

This type approach can be extremely useful not only as a teaching method but in identifying and isolating guest protection subjects about which the employee has questions or is indeed ignorant.

Behavior modeling   A takeoff on the role-playing technique, behavior modeling takes the approach that repeated behavior under directed circumstances reinforces that behavior. This process is geared to specific workplace situations. The training session typically begins with a discussion of the situation to be portrayed and a discussion of the expected learning objective.

Useful examples: Like related methods and like the examples cited in the paragraphs above, this approach can be extremely helpful when used in a situation-specific circumstance. The staged situation might be one of a person walking down a corridor and it is not known if he is a guest or an unauthorized intruder. The executive housekeeper plays out the role of interviewing correctly the person to determine his status. Employees, then, are invited to imitate the behavior which the role model executive housekeeper has portrayed.

Behavior modeling can be adopted into literally any department, often with the department head acting as the role model and performing exactly the behavior desired, having the employees mimic this behavior until there is satisfaction that the behavior is well instilled.

Case Study Members of the group are presented with a guest protection problem, preferably in written form, and are requested to discuss it, analyze it, and come up with solutions.

> Useful Examples: The group might be presented with a situation in which they are assigned on the property at night and the MOD receives word that there is a possible criminal on the property. The group leader can add or detract circumstances which change the scenario and bring into focus the possible threats involved and the possible solutions.

INDIVIDUAL TRAINING METHODS

On-the-job training This is essentially a method of training best described as learning by doing. It is the most common of all lodging training generally and certainly the most common training method insofar as guest protection training is concerned.

NOTE: The American Society for Training and Development-- ASTD--has published a guide entitled *How To Train Managers* which provides guidelines on how to equip managers with the skills necessary to conduct on-the-job training within their individual departments. It may be purchased for a nominal sum from: ASTD, 1630 Duke Street, Box 1443, Alexandria, VA 22313 (703) 683-8129.

Buddy System This is a tried and true variation of the on-the-job training method and involves a one-on-one approach. Typically an experienced employee who has been at the same property for an extended period of time is assigned to "coach" a new employee.

Useful examples: Perhaps the most common example of the buddy system is that used in the housekeeping department when an experienced room attendant is assigned a new employee to coach.

Insofar as guest protection training is concerned, parallel examples can be cited. In the case of the more experienced room attendant employing the buddy system with a new employee, a "staged" circumstance might be one in which the room is being attended to and a person from the hall tries to move the cart from the door and gain entrance. The more experienced room attendant "walks" the less experienced employee through the desired behavior.

Coaching Coaching differs from other forms of individual training methods. It is designed to address a specific desired change in behavior.

Useful examples: A front desk supervisor who is "coaching" a trainee can effectively monitor behavior while that trainee completes the registrations and assigns the appropriate guest room key. Should the trainee forget and verbalize the room number, the supervisor can take immediate action, recall that key, assign another one correctly and immediately "coach" the trainee on the desired and necessary behavior.

DOCUMENTATION

In virtually all training, there is a need for documentation.

In a classroom setting, documentation is required for proper grading and placement of students. In industry, documentation assists in verification for the job and for promotion. In the lodging industry (and other industry groups in which public access is a consideration) an additional documentation factor comes in to play--that of liability exposure.

We began this chapter by stressing that of all the eight countermeasures none was more effective or important than that of a well-trained staff.

There are examples, time and time again, in civil litigation in which the verdict has been favorable to the hotel because of testimony which showed that the entire staff was committed to guest protection.

Bellpersons testifying that they had been well trained in and were committed to guest protection carry considerable weight in a civil trial.

Room attendants testifying that they were continually trained by an executive housekeeper in proper guest protection methodology is extremely impressive to a jury.

Front desk clerks testifying that they had guest protection techniques constantly drummed into them can make the difference between winning and losing in court!

Even when a mistake has occurred--an unauthorized person admitted to guestroom for instance, or a front desk clerk mistakenly verbalizing a room number, juries can still be forgiving! Juries are made up of a cross section of the population and they understand an inadvertent mistake or occasional slip of an individual employee.

What they will not accept is a property which did not train that employee well and effectively in the first place.

And there is no better method of showing, in court, that such training was conducted well and effectively than the presentation of training documentation.

POINTS TO PONDER

GUEST PROTECTION TRAINING

◆   Examine the position taken in the text that staff-wide guest protection training is vital.

◆   List departments in a typical property the employees of which should receive guest protection training in each of the following countermeasures:

*   Pre-employment
*   Access control
*   Lighting
*   Key control
*   Protection officers
*   Guestroom protection
*   Emergency response
*   Determine which employees, *if any,* should not receive training in each of the countermeasures listed above.
*   Discuss the importance of documenting training.

CHAPTER TEN

ACCESS CONTROL

Access control is that countermeasure designed to limit, monitor, control or otherwise influence the movement of persons and vehicles onto, from, and within a property.

Examples of access control abound--fences, doors, signs, speed bumps. Like other countermeasures, it is generally not *absolute* but rather *relative and complimentary.*

A five-foot block fence around the perimeter of a hotel, for instance, is an obvious and often very effective example of the use of access control. The control which this barrier causes is, however, by no means absolute. Let's look at it.

> A five-foot block wall can be scaled with ease.

> There are breaks within the wall (gates) which can be used to neutralize its protective quality.

> With time and age, its protective strength becomes less.

None of these obvious limitations, however, detract from the fact that access control (in this case a fence) can be and usually is an effective countermeasure. Consider the several ingredients contained in the definition of access control and the applications thereof.

The limiting quality Access control is designed to *limit* access. A locked or otherwise secured door to a storage shed *limits* access. Ease of access is lessened while not absolutely preventing the unauthorized entry into that building or room.

NOTE: A significant amount of crime is committed spontaneously. That is to say it is often not well-planned or even planned in advance. Rather when the opportunity presents itself, the crime is often committed. An excellent example of this is youth vandalism. In many cases, the act of vandalism is unplanned and very costly to the property. A limiting quality within an access control system, such as the simple lock on the storage door, often keeps such spontaneous acts from occurring.

The monitoring quality Access control is designed to monitor access. A log-in sheet at a food-storage area *monitors (*and decreases, while not absolutely preventing) the unauthorized entry into that room.

The controlling quality   Access control is designed to *control* access. An electronic access code used in conjunction with a touch pad to a restricted area *controls* (while not absolutely preventing) the unauthorized entry into that area.

The influencing quality Access control is designed to *otherwise influence* access and the movement of people or vehicles. Perhaps the most obvious example of such successful influencing is the simple use of gender signs on restroom doors!

It is obvious then from these and other examples that access control is a relative countermeasure. It is also complementary. That is to say, its effectiveness can be enhanced by its use in concert with other countermeasures and by adjusting the control features with the countermeasure itself. Consider the following as compliments or adjustments to the situations described above.

The limiting features of access control   While locking or otherwise securing the door of a storage shed provides a certain level of protection, the requirement that a roving protection officer intermittently check the building increases the access control protection level.

The monitoring features of access control   While the requirement that a person entering a restricted food storage area sign in and out, the addition of a time-lapse camera which records such entries obviously makes the access control stronger.

The control features of access control   The protective features of having an electronic touch pad access to a severely restricted area can be further increased, for instance, by frequent and well-monitored changes to the access code.

The influencing features of access control   The example of the gender signs on restrooms is an excellent illustration of how specific access control techniques can overtly (and often subliminally) influence those whom we are trying to affect.

TECHNIQUES AND METHODS OF ACCESS CONTROL

A written policy on access control should be considered, directing responsibility for maintenance, inspection and intermittent adequacy assessments.

We have seen that access control attempts to limit, monitor, control and otherwise influence the movement onto, from and within a property of pedestrian and vehicular traffic.   Many techniques and methods may be utilized successfully in this endeavor.   Again, as is the case of all countermeasures, access control is property-specific and the methods and techniques utilized must be similarly individualized.

The examples which follow may be used as guides and benchmarks from which to develop such a personalized access control system.   As these examples are presented, the term access control is used broadly and is meant to either incorporate any or all of the incremental ingredients (limiting, monitoring, controlling or influencing) or concentrate on only one.

THE ACCESS CONTROL OF VEHICULAR TRAFFIC

Access control of vehicular traffic begins at the entrance or entrances to the property. In the case of those properties which are located away from and out of sight of the main thoroughfares, access control sometimes begins off the property.

In most instances, with the exception of exclusive resort properties, the entrances to the property are unmonitored. Signs are the most used access control devices at these points. They continue into and throughout the property and are usually effective.

VEHICULAR ACCESS CONTROL SIGNS

Restricted access signs Many properties post signs at the perimeter vehicular access points which enthusiastically welcome guests, and direct vendors. At the same time, these signs discourage unauthorized entrance. "No trespassing, except authorized guests or employees" signs placed at little used or limited access points are often effective.

NOTE: Managers should refer to and be consistent with local ordinances and statutes when designing and posting such signs. Often the ability to prosecute trespassers is dependent on the proper wording and placement of such signs.

Directional signs Guests driving onto the property often   require directions to the registration area. Clear, readable and attractive signs provide that needed service. Vendors and suppliers, likewise, require direction to their authorized destination. If the hours which property can accommodate vendors and suppliers are restricted or limited, this information, too, will assist in the orderly conduct of business.

Speed and other limiting signs Speed must be controlled, and the normal method of such control is speed limit signs. Attention should be given to specific areas of greatest concern--pedestrian crossings,

184

playground areas and areas of possible traffic obstruction or danger. Particular attention should be given to the lighting or reflective quality of speed limit signs.

NOTE: Coordination with local regulatory agencies should be affected when planning or posting speed limit signs.

Additional vehicular-control limiting signs include signs which announce traffic direction (one-way signs) limitation on turns (No Right Turn) and signs which announce destination limitations (dead-end or no-access to the main thoroughfare.)

Warning or cautionary signs   Motorists should be warned of possible dangers and situations which require their special attention. Sudden turns in the driveway, dangerous cross traffic, heavy equipment or truck traffic and pedestrian crossings are but a few of the examples which should be addressed.

Informational signs   Special attractions, times of operation and events are often highlighted by the use of both permanent and temporary signs.

VEHICULAR   ACCESS   CONTROL   DEVICES   AND
TECHNIQUES

Designated Parking   Designated parking, especially for employees, is a major access control consideration. Developing, using and *enforcing* employee parking has several advantages:

It maximizes available designated space for guest parking.

It allows for better attention to employee personal protection.

It reduces the likelihood of employee theft.

It allows for better control and safety of employee vehicles.

Speed control devices   Speeded bumps, when strategically placed, *carefully and prominently announced,* are often very effective in controlling speed in designated areas such as long, uninterrupted driveways or pedestrian crossings.

Roadway dividers/traffic cones   These are useful for semi-permanent or temporary traffic control issues. Further, the use of gate barriers , such as chains or heavy rope, can be an effective and inexpensive method of temporary access control.

NOTE: The department responsible for placing such temporary barriers should be aware that vision of such devices is often difficult at night and therefore appropriate lighting/vision adjustments must be considered.

Tire barriers   Devices designed to allow only one-way designated travel of vehicles are effective but should be used sparingly and carefully. Not only are the diagonally- positioned teeth a hazard in and of themselves, but inadvertent   damage   to   tires   is   not uncommon.

Card access devices   These devices used most often for selected parking areas are less common in the lodging industry than in others. They are useful, however when circumstances dictate, but their expense (and possible morale problem) should be considered.

Signage   Signs which control access to dangerous areas such as electrical rooms should be carefully designed and placement should be in keeping with code. They should be used in conjunction with locking devices.

Directional signs are appropriate for directing pedestrian traffic to desired destinations such as recreational areas and meeting rooms.

Warning signs are vital when temporary or ongoing hazards exist (wet floors, construction, renovations, pool restrictions, etc.)

NOTE: Managers should verify the wording and placement of such signs with existing codes.

PEDESTRIAN ACCESS CONTROL DEVICES AND TECHNIQUES

<u>Alarms</u>   Perhaps the most common and useful technique of pedestrian access control is that of alarms and other electronic and mechanical deterrent devices.   When such devices are used or considered, appropriate safeguards are essential. The maintenance department should assure appropriate U.L. or Factory Mutual approval and proper code-compliance.

Perimeter and broad area protection devices, while common in many industry groups, are less so in the lodging industry.   Some applications exist, however, including the alarming of perimeter gates, usually installed with a central station annunciating capacity. Application is also not uncommon in protecting pool areas during off-hours.

Point of entry devices are more commonly used in protecting window and door access points which cannot be otherwise monitored. Such devices are often hard wired to a central annunciation point and allow response when intrusion is attempted.

In other circumstances, simple local alarm devices sound at the point of attempted intrusion. Several versions and approaches are possible depending on the circumstance--glass breakage devices; contact devices; heat sensor and movement devices all examples. The sophistication and capability of these devices increase consistent with their cost.

Restricting *exit* pedestrian traffic at designated doors is another example of access control and provides an effective and relatively inexpensive way of restricting access to designated doors which cannot otherwise be monitored.

Some are simple local alarms which annunciate when unauthorized access is attempted, but this approach is often inappropriate because of the effect which such noise has on guests.

Another softer approach, although more expensive, is hard wiring such alarms to a central annunciation point from which appropriate response can be dispatched. Obviously the decision regarding the type and placement of door alarms will be steeped in circumstances.

<u>Camera</u>   Surveillance cameras are not an uncommon approach to access control. They can be useful but their use and appropriateness depends on the circumstance for which they were designed.

Surveillance cameras, for instance, are not usually an effective access control tool when immediate response is required. There are several reasons for this limitation in effectiveness. Not only must a constant and alert capability be maintained at the monitoring point, but also situation diagnosis is often difficult to accomplish. Additionally, response capability and time are often inadequate. Better uses of surveillance cameras are in those instances when a recording backup exists and can later be appropriately viewed and diagnosed.

<u>Badges</u>   Vendor and contractor badging procedures either in conjunction with their sign-in/sign-out requirements or used independently are often appropriate. Not only do they provide a retainable documentation of visits, they act in and of themselves as a deterrent to unauthorized entry.

The decision to utilize employee badges is a major one. As a rule-of-thumb it is encouraged for several reasons:

* It provides a method for guests to easily identify employees.

* Badges can be used for time and attendance purposes as well as for identification.

* If badges are issued on a daily basis, the system provides for a quick check on attendance levels.

* Different coded or colored badges are useful for department and/or area access authorization.

* Badges provide ease of access control when a discharge or termination situation takes place.

* Badges are available in a great variety of designs, materials and uses.

Management is well advised to plan carefully prior to selecting a badging system. The issues for consideration include initial and replacement cost (both time and money), the use for which the proposed system is anticipated, and the appearance of the badge itself.

Employee Entrances   The use of employee entrances (often in conjunction with employee parking areas) can be an effective access control method. It offers several advantages:

* If properly designed and enforced, employee entrances can channel and restrict employees to desired designated areas.

* It can facilitate and strengthen time and attendance procedures.

* It can minimize exposure of employees to hazards.

* It can reduce employee theft.

Involvement of employees in access control can neither be overlooked nor overemphasized. Elsewhere in this text there is reference to the importance of having employees become de facto protection officers. When they do so, they are usually performing an access control function and such efforts should be a part of the employee training scheme described in chapter nine.

In guestroom situations, particularly, employees should be encouraged and directed to encounter or report any person who has the appearance and mannerisms of being "out of the ordinary" or whose movements and body language suggest being lost, confused, or "suspicious."

Obviously, if such a situation in any way suggests danger, the employee must be trained to call a predetermined person or department. When the employee is comfortable in a direct encounter, such should be encouraged. Approaching a person with a friendly, smiling demeanor and asking, "May I help you?" is a scenario which rarely is taken any way but positively.

By reporting to predesignated persons or departments the appearance of persons who appear to be unauthorized, crime can often be deterred. In the event that a person or group is encountered who turns out to be authorized, the mere fact of having encountered them tends to "put them on notice" and the likelihood of subsequent in appropriate behavior is decreased.

Public areas, particularly in larger properties with extensive grounds, provide fertile invitations to unauthorized persons, most often youths. The same training of employees is appropriate in anticipation of these circumstances.

POINTS TO PONDER

ACCESS CONTROL

◆   Define access control as a countermeasure.

◆   List several countermeasures which can be used as compliment to access control.

◆   List a countermeasure which might possibly be acceptable *in the absence* of effective access control.

◆   Examine and discuss the position that access control is a relative rather than an absolute countermeasure.

◆   Identify which of the four threats to guests which may be impacted by effective access control.

◆   Identify which, if any, of the four threats which exist to guests *may* not be impacted by effective access control.

◆   Defend the position that advisory signs are effective access control tools.

◆   Discuss access control measures which may be *easily and inexpensively* developed and introduced by local property management.

CHAPTER ELEVEN

LIGHTING

Lighting has been used as an effective countermeasure since the taming and early use of fire by our ancestors. Man learned early on that dangers existed at night which did not exist during the light of day. By applying light, a portion of these dangers could be neutralized.

Virtually every professional crime prevention authority agrees on the value of lighting as a deterrent. Studies performed in rural and urban centers, in industrial and residential districts, in virtually any and all settings, showed beyond a reasonable doubt that lighting is a deterrent to crime. This fact is no less true in the lodging industry.

* Lighting decreases the likelihood of crime in parking lots.

* Lighting decreases the likelihood of crime in hallways and corridors.

* Lighting decreases the likelihood of crime in storage areas.

* Lighting decreases the likelihood of crime at access points to buildings.

And the advantages of the presence of lighting are not limited to a protection standpoint or to the deterrence of crime. Proper lighting is unquestionably a factor in accident reduction as well. Slip-and-fall incidents decrease with proper lighting. In the maintenance and engineering areas, accidents decrease with proper lighting. Sufficient lighting can have a positive effect on guest safety and satisfaction with guestrooms.

Given these favorable aspects of lighting, one would think lighting would be an indispensable and widely-used countermeasure in every lodging setting. Perhaps it should be, but very practical problems exist.

Lighting is often extremely expensive. Not only can the uncontrolled use of lighting greatly affect the profitability of a property, but the initial installation can be a major undertaking and the maintenance required to insure continuing proper application also can be a burden.

Another inherent problem with lighting often presents itself. Managers at the property level usually find themselves faced with a lighting situation over which they had little or no initial input. The property may have been several years or decades old when the managers began employment. The initial style, type, placement, design, and intensity are conditions with which the manager must deal and over which they have little control.

The dual challenges, therefore, of this countermeasure being both costly and difficult to manage sometimes cause the lodging manager to shy away from it as an effective crime-control measure.

This propensity to overlook or ignore this very useful countermeasure should be avoided. While the manager may have limited ability to influence the placement, illuminating capabilities and style of lighting on the property, he does have the obligation to address the subject with whatever latitude he possesses.

LIGHTING CONSIDERATIONS

Policy   A written policy regarding lighting should be considered. This policy might describe required maintenance, including preventive maintenance. It should include inspection schedules and an intermittent audit of the documented work order trail from the time a malfunction originally occurred until the problem is expeditiously rectified.

Code requirements Local, county, and state codes with regard to lighting are many and varied. Management should establish both an initial and scheduled ongoing procedures. One may expect (and should welcome) jurisdictional inspections by agencies such as OSHA, etc. Their findings should be acted upon as quickly as possible and both their visits and the property's response should be well documented.

NOTE: Insofar as the sufficiency of lighting is concerned, there is no known national standard. A rule-of-thumb which is often applied is that of attempting to read a newspaper in any given lighted area. If the paper can be read, the lighting is sufficient.

Area coverage The areas of most common concern include: the perimeter, access points, broad open areas, parking lots and garages, driveways and commonly-used walkways.

Perimeter The perimeter of the property, depending again on the particular configuration, should be examined from a lighting standpoint.

Diagnostically, the existence and effectiveness of such lighting will be determined during the property survey. (See chapter six.) However, the effectiveness of the lighting and its proper balance in concert with other appropriate countermeasures such as access control will be developed during the examination and analysis by the protection management committee.

Access points Access points, both pedestrian and vehicular, at the perimeter and at the exterior of commonly used buildings should receive appropriate lighting attention. Crime deterrence is of particular concern in such settings.

Broad open areas   Often less concentrated lighting is appropriate in these locations, but aesthetics and limited places where criminals could easily hide are considerations in these lighting decisions.

Parking lots and garages   Parking areas present classic challenges insofar as guest protection is concerned and lighting is normally required. Again, the decision on lighting should be made only after the diagnostic survey has been completed and the findings can be reviewed in conjunction with other appropriate countermeasures.

Driveways and commonly used walkways   In these locations, like commonly used entry ways, the use of appropriate amounts of lighting is important. Crime as well as accidents can be deterred when lighting efforts illuminate such otherwise dark and dangerous areas.

MOD responsibility   Frequent and documented grounds inspection, including a study particular to lighting is appropriate in those properties where such can be accomplished.

Maintenance department responsibility   Normally the maintenance department conducts or directs the installation, maintenance and adjustment of lighting. Maintenance and adjustment should be accomplished on a scheduled basis and such maintenance should be documented. Work orders for lighting maintenance, like all guest protection related work order requests, should be addressed in a timely manner.

In many cases preventive maintenance has been found to be both operationally and economically effective. By replacing, for instance, entire banks or section of lights on a carefully timed and scheduled basis, labor cost savings may surpass the replacement cost of the lights even if they have not yet burned out.

<u>Protection officers' responsibility</u> If protection officers are utilized, lighting inspections should be an expected part of their scheduled or random rounds. Discovery of lighting malfunctions should appear on their patrol log and an appropriate work order submitted. Verification should be made that the work order has been received by maintenance and the work is being accomplished expeditiously.

<u>Bell staff, F&B and housekeeping staff responsibilities</u> Employees in any and all departments who, in the course of their work, are in a position to view lighting, should be responsible for reporting instances of lighting malfunctions.

This responsibility should obviously include instances of inoperative lighting but it should not end there. Instances of "troublesome" areas (e.g., pockets of darkness) should likewise be reported and the appropriate work order request submitted. Follow up and verification should be accomplished.

<u>Interior hallway lighting</u> Depending on the configuration of the property, hallway lighting can be used effectively not only as a crime deterrence measure but additionally as a safety and aesthetic consideration.   During the surveys and subsequent evaluation of lighting, the GM, as well as the Protection Management Committee, is assured of adequacy.

<u>Emergency lighting</u> Emergency lighting is often covered by regulation or code and compliance with such directives is, of course, an absolute requirement. Beyond or in addition to whatever code requirements exist, emergency lighting considerations should be given to placement, capability, intensity, inspections and repair.

As is the case with virtually all such countermeasures, documentation should be accomplished and retained.

POINTS TO PONDER

LIGHTING

◆   Identify other countermeasures which compliment, or are complimented by, lighting.

◆   Identify at least four locations on a typical property where effective lighting may be critical.

◆   Identify and discuss the two generally accepted reasons which may cause lighting to be the countermeasure least "useable and adaptable" by the Innkeeper.

◆   Discuss the common rule-of-thumb for determining the adequacy of exterior lighting.

◆   Discuss typical MOD responsibility regarding lighting.

◆   Discuss typical protection officer responsibility regarding lighting.

◆   Discuss typical bell staff, F&B and housekeeping responsibility regarding lighting.

CHAPTER TWELVE

KEY CONTROL

The control of keys within the lodging industry is essential.

This is a simple, straightforward and virtually universal truth and bears repeating.

The control of keys within the lodging industry is essential.

Trial attorneys proficient in premises liability exposure suggest that of all "glitches" which doom Innkeepers in civil lawsuits wherein inadequate security has been alleged, the lack of appropriate key control probably is the most common.

And yet, while perhaps few hoteliers would disagree with the *theoretical* validity of this statement, many do not accept it in practice. There appears to be one overriding reason for this less than universal buy-in into key control, and that is the perception that as a continuing and effective countermeasure to crime, it is futile.

For no reason other than the sheer volume of keys with which a hotel manager must deal, the problem of key control may be seen as overwhelming. In the face of this perception, however, two facts emerge which should mitigate temptations to ignore or mismanage key control.

Key control *can*, indeed, be accomplished, and

Key control *must*, indeed, be accomplished!

A look at the state-of-the-art in guestroom keying is in order and will shed some light, not on the predisposition of some to shun this countermeasure, but on a new dimension of its viability.

Perhaps no aspect of hotel management has experienced the growth and technological change within the past few decades as that of guestroom locking devices.

There are countless hoteliers active today who well remember the common use of the term "pass key." In today's lodging technological environment, such a word seems archaic, but even today, the use of such devices as key-in-knob locking systems and simple interior guestroom door hooks are not unheard of!

It is true that a vast number of smaller properties do not have the means to upgrade guestroom locking systems to a level many larger properties accept as a given. *What must be stressed, however, is that regardless of the inherent level of effectiveness of a guestroom locking system, the requirement for key control within that system remains firm.*

ISSUES AND CONSIDERATIONS

Key control should be viewed, not unlike PEV and other hotel protection countermeasures, as a *process.*

Further, not only is it a process, it is anything but a linear process. On the contrary, the process of key control, while perhaps not perfectly circular, has no specific beginning and certainly no specific end. It involves a continuous series of actions, controls, requirements, and validations. It involves virtually every department on the property.

And finally, it is multi-layered. An explanatory prologue to the subject of key control and a discussion of the focus of this text is in order.

This chapter will be devoted to key control as such a process, and will examine during the discussion of the various levels of keys, the following elements:

* Key production
* Key storage
* Key issuance
* Key retrieval
* Key inventory

Each of these five elements will be examined as the process of key control is viewed during its "circular" process route.

The thrust of this examination will be twofold.   First, it will concentrate on those keying systems which are mechanical and second, it will further focus exclusively on the guestroom.   The reasons follow:

Mechanical systems   The lodging industry is well aware that locking and keying technology has grown at a staggering pace over the past few decades.   Such advance continues and it is a rare lodging magazine which does not advertise yet another newer and more advanced level of locking and key technology.

Of further significance is the fact that virtually without exception the training in and maintenance of the key control aspect of such systems is a part of the offering.

As such, the buyer receives not only a state-of-the-art system, but also instruction and training in its use. Those vast numbers of properties still relying on mechanical systems have no such advantage. It is for the reader associated with those properties, that this chapter is particularly appropriate and specifically aimed.

Guestroom key focus   This chapter is devoted almost exclusively to that portion of key control which concerns itself with the *guestroom*.

While the term "key control" may convey a countermeasure which is property-wide, the thrust of this text is *guest* (rather than any other asset) *protection*. Back-of-the-house key control, therefore, while admittedly important is not the thrust.

KEY LEVELS

Most hoteliers agree that there are three distinct and identifiable levels of guestroom keys, ranging both in criticality and the need for protection and control. These levels include the emergency key (**E Key**), the master key and the guestroom keys.

Each is vital to the successful operation of the property. Each should be examined and understood in terms of its place on the key hierarchy and each must be afforded specific protection.

The Emergency Key   Commonly called the E Key, the emergency key is defined as "that key which can both unlock a double locked door and double lock an unlocked door."

The Master Key   Usually one of several, the master key is defined as "that key which can open all rooms (in our context meaning guestrooms) which are not double locked.

The Guestroom Key   This key is defined as "the key designed to open a specific guestroom which is not double locked."

THE E KEY

The simple and concise definition of the E Key cited above tends to disguise the importance of this device. Consider the fact that this key is figuratively (and in some sense literally) the "key to the vault."

Consider that a guest, following advice given him on a guestroom posting, double locks his door by depressing the button located in the

202

center of the inside guestroom doorknob. His belief is that he is virtually as secure within that double-locked room as a guest can become. What he may not realize, however, *and what highlights the importance of protection for the E key* is the fact that anyone with that E Key can bypass the double lock and enter that otherwise secure room. Keys to the vault indeed!

There are several approaches to E Key protection. Limiting the number of E Keys is, in and of itself, a protective measure. There are properties which limit themselves to one and only one E Key. At one notable seminar, the seminar leader discussed this limiting of keys. He then, however, was informed by one GM in the audience that he (the GM) had authorized the production of 25 E Keys for his 200 room property, one of which he had in his pocket at this far-distant city!

The production of the E Key should be under the highest of controlled circumstances. Production authorization should be limited to a minimum of senior management personnel and such production stringently monitored and documented.

Issuance, like production, should be highly controlled and permitted only by the signature of the same limited number of senior management personnel. Unfortunately, possession of the E Key often becomes a status symbol, being in the mind of the holder tangible proof of his elevated and important position and functions.

Engineers, for example, often claim an absolute need for the E Key. Careful analysis of the rational for that stated need will often disclose that convenience (and perhaps ego) are usually the driving forces.

Control and availability of the E Key are both vital and inherent in its designed use. As the name implies, the "emergency key" is designed for emergency use. Consider the front desk or telephone operator receiving a call from a gasping guest who indicates chest pain. Such an occurrence (smoke or fire would be another instance) constitutes the type emergency in which the E Key is to be used. In preparation for, as well as during, such emergencies, the following controls and principles should apply to and surround the E Key.

(1)   The E Key must provide access to all locked guestroom doors. Additionally, some properties and indeed some political jurisdictions operate in modes whereby the E Key also provides access to all emergency-related doors   such as electrical and boiler rooms, elevator access, and fire-alarm panels.

(2)   While the E Key must be maintained in the safest and most secure manner possible, it also must be available for obvious reasons at a moment's notice. Normally such availability is made to front desk personnel, *but on a controlled and recorded basis.*

The E Key should be safely stored, ideally in a locked but accessible mode (e.g., a glass container, the door of which must be broken to access the key.)

When use is necessary, a record should be made of the date, time, circumstance of the use as well as the identity of all personnel having access during that emergency.   This backup documentation should be retained and security   stored for an extended period of time.

(3)   Some properties, even though they maintain an absolute minimum number of E Keys (perhaps only the one available to the front desk) have found that a second E Key securely maintained in the property safe and inventoried on a   regular basis provides effective and sufficient backup.

(4)   Other than legitimate emergencies, no other use of the E Key should be permitted.

(5)   There is no known justification for an E Key ever being permitted to leave a property.

When the issue of guest protection and reasonable care is raised in a civil law suit, there is perhaps no more damning evidence suggesting the <u>absence</u> of such levels than that of having given insufficient protection to this most vital tool.

In summary, the E Key should receive the highest protection and control available and possible.

THE MASTER KEY

As shown earlier, a master key is designed to allow access to guestroom doors which have not been double locked, as well as to selected other locked rooms within a given area. There are levels of master keys, depending on the size and configuration of the property.

(1)   Grand Masters (and in some cases "great grand masters") which are designed to open all doors on the property except double-locked guestroom doors. The use of these masters is becoming less and less common because of their vulnerability and the increased use of sub- or section- or building masters.

(2)   Sub masters, as the name implies, are subordinate to grand master keys and are designed to access all doors, except guestroom double locked doors *in a given area.* Building masters, for instance, may access all such doors within a given building; floor masters may access such doors on a given floor, etc.

Like the E Key, strict controls and accountability are required for master keys.

Whenever possible, masters should be subdivided into sub-masters. The loss or compromise of a sub-master is less serious or expensive to counteract than that of a master key. Assignment and accountability, too, support the division of masters into sub-masters. (The sales staff may have a legitimate reason to have a sub-master to a given guest room but certainly not the more unrestricted access required by a room attendant in that same building or on that same floor.)

Sub-mastering and related appropriate issues and control procedures take into account this uneven access reality and allow for area as well as personnel departmental issuance.

Master keys should be accessible from limited sources. Often, they should be accessible, as is the E Key, only from the front desk.

On some properties masters have been permanently issued to key senior management personnel, such as the executive housekeeper. Even in these cases, however, the overnight or off-duty storage and control of the master is usually best assigned to the front desk.

Irrespective of the location chosen for such a control point, the masters should be securely locked in a key cabinet or some other equally secure device and access/accountability carefully maintained.

Issuance of the master keys from the central control point should be in conformance with a system carefully designed and constantly monitored.

Periodic review of persons authorized to *issue* as well as *receive* such keys is important. And issuance should be on a signature basis, limited to persons specifically identified by senior management. The key return likewise should be authenticated and inventory taken, ideally on a daily basis.

Procedure should be in effect to immediately react when the inventory discloses a discrepancy. The documentation which verifies the issuance, return and inventory of master keys should be maintained and stored for an appropriate period of time.

Coding (not specific identification) is often successfully employed by hotels in their master key control system. For example, by using a color code tag system, one color may indicate departmental sub-masters and another color might indicate floor or building or section sub-masters. Such a tagging system aids in inventory control, issuance, and storage.

As with the E keys. master keys should never be allowed to leave the property.

THE GUESTROOM KEY

Guestroom keys are the lowest level of the three-level tier. Guestroom keys, obviously, are those keys produced which provide access to a particular guestroom door. They should open the door of the particular guestroom for which they were designed and produced *and no other.*

Like the E Key and the master keys, centralized control of the guestroom keys is normally maintained at a central location, usually the front desk.

A key "par" should be established and the number of keys below par should trigger appropriate re-coring, re-keying, hardware rotation and/or production of replacement keys. The number of keys which constitute "par" is a matter of individual management decision but the adage that less is usually better is certainly apropos.

Markings or fobs or engravings on the guestroom key should not identify the property. Room identification is best handled by eliminating the room identification from the key and supplying the key to the guest in a packet, card, or envelope on which is written the room number.

Storage of the guestroom keys at the front desk should be in a secured drawer or cabinet, out of the view and access of everyone other than authorized personnel.

THE PROCESS -- THE CIRCULAR ROUTE OF KEY CONTROL AND ACCOUNTABILITY

The three departments most involved in the key control process are the front desk, housekeeping and maintenance. A discussion of the role of these three departments follows and then a discussion of the involvement of all persons and departments which normally play a role in the guestroom key control process.

The Front Desk The "beginning" of the circular route is the front desk. This department, generally speaking, is the focal point of the circular path which the guestroom keys will take throughout the property. Training of the front desk staff in the key control policies and procedures is essential if success is to be realized. This training should be a continuing process.

Inventory of guestroom keys should be a matter of course and on a regular and scheduled basis, at least once daily. The ideal time for such inventory is often immediately after checkout time and appropriate inventory forms should be completed promptly. Housekeeping, then should be placed into the inventory loop so that keys recovered by that department are considered. If re-keying, re-coring or rotation is appropriate, the affected guestrooms absolutely should be placed out of service by management until this is accomplished.

Guestroom keys are to be issued to registered guests only, normally at the time of registration. A method of recording the number of keys issued should be adopted and additional authorized issuance, should also be noted so that reconciliation can be made upon checkout.

Both positive identification and authority must be obtained prior to issuing additional keys. Additionally, guestroom numbers should never be audibly announced by the issuing front desk clerk.

When checkout occurs, the front desk should remind each guest to return his key. *This practice is simple, can be polite and non-assertive, and can be an extremely effective method of key retrieval. However, it often is not utilized.*

If the departing guest indicates his key or keys have been left at the guestroom, he should be assured that is perfectly acceptable and that housekeeping will retrieve the key during cleaning.

On the other hand, often the guest has his key in his pocket and a simple courteous comment will serve as a reminder.

When the front desk is alerted that a situation has occurred which might impact from a protection standpoint on the key control process, corrective action is called for immediately. Such procedures would be a part of the overall key control procedure and a continuing part of the training.

Front desk responsibility normally extends beyond guestroom key control into both master key and E Key control. Both these types of keys should be inventoried on a regular basis, at least once daily.

The ideal time for this inventory is often late afternoon when most of the master and sub-master keys have been returned to inventory. This recurring inventory, like the guestroom key inventory, should be appropriately recorded on an inventory form and properly stored according to established policy.

Housekeeping The housekeeping staff normally is the next department to become involved in the key control process. During the daily process of cleaning guestrooms, room attendants will normally retrieve several keys which have been left, inadvertently or by design, by departing guests.   Ideally a locked box securely attached to the housekeeping cart should be utilized to store these retrieved keys until delivery at the end of the shift. A responsible person should be assigned to transport all retrieved keys shortly after the end of the shift, back to the front desk so that they can be entered into the inventory

Strict rules prohibiting the access of *anyone* to locked guestroom doors should be established and rigidly enforced. Room attendants should be instructed that requests from *anyone* to enter a locked guestroom door should be referred to the front desk or to senior management.

Master keys should be secured on the room attendant's person at all times. Chains which allow both such security and required access are usually successful.

Maintenance The maintenance department could be labeled as that point on the "circular" key-control route where all things begin.

While from the guest's standpoint the front desk is where the process begins, in actuality, it is in the maintenance department that the process has its roots. This is normally where the initial production occurs with the cutting of guestroom keys from the stored key blanks. This awesome responsibility, the ability to duplicate virtually any guestroom key at any moment, causes special attention to be focused on the maintenance department.

Key-cutting machinery should be well stored, controlled, and access limited. This machinery should be stored in a secure area, either in a room to which access can be rigidly controlled or if this is not feasible, then sub-compartmentalized in a secured cabinet. Access to the controlled room or the secure storage location should be by designated persons only.

Key blanks should be controlled by a designated level of management--often the chief engineer or maintenance department manager. Storing these blanks and securing them independently from the key-cutting device and limiting access to them by designated management personnel allows for an effective audit method for security purposes. A running inventory of these blanks provides for assurance of control.

An audit method, (a paper trail) should be established and maintained. It should be rigidly monitored and validated on a frequent and scheduled basis.

Normally guestroom key duplication requests come exclusively from the front desk and are printed in multiples allowing copies to be maintained at specific locations along the production and issuance path. The procedure as well as the format of the key request should provide and insure control at all locations along the circular route. The request form should indicate the reason for the request (e.g., a key cannot be accounted for and re-keying is required or a key has been damaged or is flawed and replacement is required.)

Master and sub-master key reproduction requires special controls. Obviously a misplaced master or sub-master requires immediate attention, not only to replace the key but more importantly to re-key effected doors to which the misplaced master allowed access.

Authority for such duplication and the adherence to quick and reliable re-keying should be vested in a predetermined level of management. Adherence to the required rapid re-keying in this situation is essential and should be audited on a frequent basis.

Other departments, employees and circumstances involved in the guestroom key control process follow.

(1)   When a bellperson escorts a guest to his room, he should be certain that the guestroom key is functioning properly and that the guest understands how the key operates.

NOTE: As discussed in the training chapter, the bellperson should familiarize the guest with all protection devices in the room and demonstrate them if appropriate.

(2)   If a bellperson assists a guest during checkout, the bellperson would remind the guest that the key is to be returned and that he, the bellperson, can assist if that is desired. The retrieved key is then obviously returned to the front desk.

(3)   Issuance of keys to the bell and valet staff should normally be controlled at the front desk.

(4)   Van and courtesy drivers should remind departing guests of the necessity of returning keys and offer to accept from them any guestroom key which might have been forgotten. A locked box, not unlike that suggested for the room attendant's cart, is useful on vans and courtesy vehicles.

(5)   All employees, irrespective of position or department, should be trained in the importance of key control. They should be aware of key control discrepancies and proper response. Such events might include such circumstances as discovering misplaced keys or becoming aware of inappropriate issuance or "borrowing" of keys.

(6)   Some properties employ a guestroom key deposit system. In such an approach, a nominal deposit is collected or announced during the registration process

and then returned or eliminated from the billing process when the key is returned. There are at least two distinct advantages to this process, 1) a reminder to the guest to return his key as well as an incentive to do so, and 2) the system also provides a money stream to offset the cost of key replacement. The principal disadvantage is the danger of poor guest relations. There is little doubt that this danger exists--guests often feel "put upon" when a deposit is required, feeling either that they are being mistrusted or that the property is taking unacceptable advantage of them.

It is important, therefore, if a key deposit system is employed, that the front desk personnel be careful and thoroughly trained and scripted in the way the system is to be presented and carried out.

At check out time, a soft approach should be used--courteously accepting the guest's explanation, for instance, that he "left his key in the room."

Obviously, if a key deposit system is employed, it must be universally applied. Intermittent use, for example, when a "suspicious" guest is being processed is unacceptable.

Finally, managers must understand that a key deposit system in no way is meant to replace a comprehensive and effective guestroom key control system.

Employees sometimes mistakenly assume that the adoption of a deposit system allows the relaxation of the overall key control process. They should be taught otherwise.

POINTS TO PONDER

KEY CONTROL

◆ Identify the five elements listed in the text which could b considered in the evaluation of effective key control.

◆ Identify and define the three levels of keys discussed in the text.

◆ Thoroughly examine and justify the position that the E Key may be considered "the key to the vault."

◆ Discuss the main concerns surrounding the protection of the E Key.

◆ List departments, employees of which may claim to require issuance of the E Key and then determine if such issuance can be justified.

◆ If you determined any permanent issue to any employee of any department is justified, examine counter-positions which would nullify such a justification and need.

◆ Identify possible acceptable E Key storage methods which would incorporate both necessary protection and accessibility.

◆　　Attempt to image a scenario in which the removal of an E Key from a property is justified and required.

◆　　If you are able to develop such a scenario, attempt to determine how the requirement and justification could be mitigated *without such a removal.*

◆　　Define the Master and sub-master keys.

◆　　List the advantages, from a guest protection standpoint, resulting from developing several sub-master keys from a single master key.

◆　　Define guestroom keys.

◆　　Define "par."

◆　　Define a typical route which a guestroom key might be expected to follow from issuance to a guest and on through the property until ready again to be issued to a newly arrived guest.

◆　　Describe the typical involvement which the front desk might have in key control.

◆　　Describe the typical involvement which the housekeeping department might have in key control.

◆　　Describe the typical involvement which the maintenance department might have in key control.

◆　　Describe the typical involvement which the bell staff might have in key control.

◆　　Identify any department which, under any circumstance would not have involvement in key control.

CHAPTER THIRTEEN

PROTECTION OFFICERS
(sometimes termed "Security Officers")

There have been two notable references thus far in this text to "security officers." In an earlier chapter, reference was made to the often-heard phrase: "Add another security guard," immediately after an incident had occurred. (Too little, too late!) An earlier chapter also hypothesized a potential guest calling a property and asking "Do you have security?" These two examples, while somewhat different in their thrust and meaning, offer an interesting insight into the countermeasure of protection officers---at least the *perception* of the countermeasure.

In both instances, the "security officer" was the first thought when the subject of protection arose. In the first case, the GM's thoughts immediately turned to the perceived need for additional security officers when an incident had occurred. In the second example, the reservations clerk, in responding to the query from a prospective guest about "security" immediately thought of and referred to "security officers" as the answer to the question.

The perception was, in both cases, that "security officers" were the only available means of providing guest protection.

The reader should accept the fact that these examples are not atypical. On the contrary, they are more common than not.

It is important, in the initial investigation of this countermeasure to determine where exactly protection officers fit. Are they (and should they be) as many managers believe, the first line of protection or are they (and should they be) far down the line of possible protection approaches?

Such an analysis is necessary if we are to give this countermeasure its due consideration. Several questions need to be posed *prior* to deciding the issue.

(1)   Why do we need (want) Security Officers? Are they necessary? Advisable? Effective?

(2)   If we need (want) them, how should they be organized? Managed? Supervised?

(3)   If we need (want) them, what should their duties be? Their authority? Should they be armed? If so, with what? Is there a liability issue which might outweigh any inherent protection we might gain?

The questions should be posed prior to any decision, but unfortunately too often they are ignored or ill-considered. It is appropriate to pose and examine each aspect of this important countermeasure.

As a departure point, it is appropriate to discuss what is expected of protection officers. While many security experts (and many lodging managers) disagree on the duties and responsibilities of protection officers, there are five basic functions which a protection officer is generally expected to perform.

(1)   Control
(2)   Patrol
(3)   Escort
(4)   Inspect
(5)   Emergency Response

<u>The control function</u> This duty, obviously, entails fulfilling management requirements of controlling activities on the property. Principal among these control considerations is that of access control

Protection officers, particularly at a fixed access point but also to some extent while on patrol, are expected to influence pedestrian as well as vehicular traffic on and around the property.

The patrol function   The patrol function includes either scheduled or unscheduled patrol of the perimeter, the grounds area, parking lots, access points and the exteriors/interiors of buildings.

Of particular concern, since the guest is the principal asset, should be patrol in areas where guests are most likely to be in need of protection--guestroom areas, commonly used walkways and access points, and recreational areas.

The escort function   This function touches on protection of the guest, the employees, and other assets. Escorts might be scheduled (at shift changes or routine bank deposits) or unscheduled (as in the need to assist a disabled guest.)

The escort function may be carried out by walking with the person to be escorted, or by supplying a vehicle, patrol car, bus, or golf cart.

The inspections function   The inspection function along with the emergency responses function is broader than the other three. We expect protection officers to inspect both on a random and scheduled basis, and further to inspect both "people" and "things." Instances of inspection might include:

> Fire inspections (ascertaining, for instance, extinguisher compliance as well as ferreting out fire hazards.)

> Safety inspections (ascertaining OSHA compliance in addition to random inspections for hazards)

> Security inspections (ascertaining property locking of doors)

This, of course, is only a partial list of the many possible inspection duties a manager may expect from his protection officers.

The emergency response function   Protection officers are traditionally thought of as the first on-property resource to call when emergencies arise.   The list of possible emergencies to which a security officer can be trained to respond includes:

Medical emergencies (e.g., responding with the capability of first aid, CPR, Heimlich maneuver.)

Fire emergencies (assessing the severity of the reported fire, calling for emergency fire equipment, acting as the initial fire fighter until such resources arrive, and crowd control and evacuation duties.)

Weather emergencies (pedestrian/vehicular control in the event of a sudden hazardous weather condition.)

Criminal emergencies (security of a crime scene pending arrival of law enforcement resources.)

There is additionally a sixth function to which some protection officers are assigned and that is a training function.

The training function   Sophisticated security departments have sometimes been given this additional task of training and such duties might include training in:

*   CPR/Heimlich maneuver
*   First aid
*   Fire extinguisher usage
*   Safety programs (e.g., training in avoiding slips/falls and common kitchen accidents)
*   Self protection (anti-rape seminars)

As the manager views these various functions *in total*, to which protection officers are traditionally assigned, he must ask himself a key question:

> "If these functions are necessary on my property, are there ways other than the use of protection officers by which these functions can be accomplished?"

If the answer is yes, then perhaps consideration should be given to *not* using protection officers as a guest protection countermeasure!

This position may well be viewed controversially by many lodging managers. However, they should consider that:

*   Protection officers are probably the most expensive countermeasure available.

*   Protection officers are often an ineffective and unreliable answer to many protection problems.

However, it should be stressed that Protection Officers, when properly selected, trained, equipped, managed and empowered, can become the most effective of all countermeasures available.

Given these potential disadvantages compared to the possible advantages of using this countermeasure, it would seem that a significant amount of thought and planning would be appropriate while making the decision to use it. Protection officers may not be required if the following conditions exist on a given property:

> If there is sufficient existing staff to accomplish the five (sometimes six) functions described above.

> If there is sufficient existing staff to act as the "eyes" and "ears" of the GM (which is another unofficial function usually used to justify the existence of a protection force.)

If the existing staff feels (with justification) that *they* are the "Protection department" and are capable and willing to carry out each of the functions *and* they are willing to testify in court to that fact.   This last aspect is vital.

Obviously, liability exposure is a major consideration when designing a protection program and installing the appropriate countermeasures. During civil liability cases, juries require reasonable care, with or without protection departments or officers. Testimony which shows that the staff itself affected such care can be as influential as the existence of a protection department.   If indeed, a staff is so trained, then protection officers may not be the countermeasure of choice.
If, on the other hand, the functions described above are deemed necessary, and existing staff is unable to fulfill those requirements, then protection officers are normally called for.   When such a decision is reached, several considerations should be addressed in order to assure the maximum protection for the investment.

These considerations include:

*   Duties and responsibilities
*   Department composition
*   Organization
*   Type of force

DUTIES AND RESPONSIBILITIES OF A LODGING SECURITY DEPARTMENT

It may seem outlandish to address and even belabor such an obvious tenet that the initial considerations in the protection department decision-making should be "duties and responsibility."   Perhaps that should be so but unfortunately it is not.

Earlier chapters have asserted that lodging managers traditionally tend to disregard protection for any number of stated reasons.

Consistent with this tendency, many managers, *even when they accepted the necessity or desirability of protection,* historically have often hired a contract security firm, given them a minimum of direction, and have been content to allow that firm to make functional decisions regarding the protection of the property.

"That's what they do for a living--let them decide" has often been the ill-advised viewpoint of the unsophisticated lodging manager. He would never think of allowing a contract agency in any *other* discipline to usurp his authority and responsibility but "Because this is their job" they allow it in this department.

It is a circumstance which the *effective* lodging manager will not allow. He, himself, needs to make these hard and important decisions, although, admittedly, they require some degree of study, reflection and investigation of often previously unfamiliar data.

He must decide if, and to what degree, this anticipated security officer force will be responsible for the basic functions described earlier.

Control Will the officers have responsibility for:

>   Fixed post locations (e.g., access points) as opposed to Patrol or both
>
>   Event and crowd control
>
>   Visitor/vendor control
>
>   Employee badging issuance and control
>
>   Employee uniform compliance

Patrol Will the officers have responsibility for:

Roving patrol duties as opposed to fixed post locations or both

Patrols which will be scheduled at random or both

Patrols which include the perimeter, and/or grounds, parking lots, specific outbuildings, public areas, guestroom area

Patrols which will require a per hour, per shift, or per day schedule

Escort Will the officers have responsibility for:

Scheduled escort services

Unscheduled escort services

Off-property escort services

Vehicular or pedestrian escort services or both

Inspection Will the officers have responsibility for:

Fire inspections (scheduled or random or both)

Safety (scheduled or random or both)

Security inspections (scheduled or random or both)

Emergency Response Will the officers have responsibility for:

Responding and rendering assistance in medical emergencies

Responding and actively counteracting in fire emergencies

Responding to severe weather emergencies

Responding to criminal emergencies

Training   Will the officers have responsibility for training staff in the following:

Medical responses (CPR/Heimlich maneuver/first aid)

Fire inspections/responses/warnings/suppression

Safety programs (safe driving, anti-slip & fall)

Self protection programs (anti-rape seminars, etc.)

This is obviously only a small portion of the issue to be determined. The important issue is that this matter constitutes and entails much more than what a manager should pass off to a contract agency with the offhanded, "It's their business; let them decide."

Even a cursory examination of this partial list should alert the most inexperienced lodging manager that protection is an established, identified and important property function and IT MUST BE MANAGED.

This, again, is a preliminary and generic list of the duties and responsibilities of a typical lodging protection force. The GM should examine the list, determine which of the duties and responsibilities he expects from his security officers, which if any additional duties and responsibility are forecast and then begin making plans for the force composition.

To the preliminary list compiled earlier in this chapter, the manager should factor in the following variables which reflect his own property.

Property location (see and incorporate the foreseeability factors discussed earlier regarding neighborhoods, crime demographics, etc.)

Neighboring lodging facilities' decision to utilize or not utilize protection officers

Property "character" (business travelers, resort, etc.)

Property size and configuration and number of rooms

Hours of operation of various departments (lounge, banquet)

Identification of particular areas of protection concern (swimming pools, stables, recreational vehicles) ?.

And, finally, what other less expensive countermeasures (from the list of seven) are to be used which can justify protection force size limitation?

DEPARTMENT COMPOSITION

Discussed on several occasions has been the unfortunate propensity of property managers to "pass off" the protection problem, often calling the first security contract agency located in the Yellow Pages. Other times, that manager may relegate the protection function almost as an afterthought to an established property department (usually maintenance or engineering.)

If a lodging manager, after the analytic review of possible protection needs outlined above, opts to establish a protection (security) force, then the same degree of management attention must go into this organizational exercise that would be expected in any departmental development.

<u>Management</u>   Once the need for a protection department is established, it should be placed on the organizational chart at a level equal to other functions. This department should report to the same level to which its sister departments report, ideally to the GM, and it should carry equal weight with those other departments.

Nearly as common as the lodging manager's propensity to "pass off" this function to an outside agency or relegate it to inferior status within existing departments is the typical decision making patter when selection of a protection manager.

Irrespective of the type of protection department chosen, and a complete discussion of the types of available protection officers follows, the necessity to establish management of that force is constant.

The question of protection department management is one often under examined. It is also common to stereotype the selection of a protection department manager. All too often this decision is ill-considered and the unfavorable consequences frequently come back to haunt that short-sighted manager. Let's consider the options that are available:

<u>A part-time manager</u> As discussed above, the relegation of the protection function to a minor role within an already existing department such as engineering is usually a mistake. If indeed the need for a protection department has been established, using the selection decision making criteria shown, then the department deserves and needs full time qualified management.

<u>Promoting from within</u>   An in-house promotion from within an existing protection force is often a desirable path to follow. The down-side, however, is often that a GM when upgrading or reestablishing a protection force, has little to choose from in terms of a potential manager. Often an existing protection department has a history of little or no attention and has fallen into an inefficient entity.

If such is the case, the GM should be very cautious when selecting a potential manager from within this group.

Selecting from outside Historically, selecting a protection manager from outside the establishment has been the most successful method. The GM who selects this option has several choices, some usually more advantageous than others.   Very often, the selection of a protection manager with a proven track record of demonstrable success is a good choice. The GM however must be wary that his prospective new employees agree with the *proactive, prevention orientation* which is desired and is not steeped in either the "Rent-A-Cop" or "Law Enforcement wanna-be" mind set, both of which are commonly found in the private security sector.

Often a former police or military official is the first (although not necessarily the best) consideration when filling this post. It is possible for such persons to successfully make the transition from the public sector to the private sector (in fact, many have!) But it is neither an easy change in thinking and behavior nor always a successful one. Consider the following:

Former or retired police officer (and perhaps the former military person) has spent a lifetime in *enforcement.*   What is called for as a Protection Manager is *prevention.*

Both the former officer and the military member have had the "power of the badge" (or rank) in both managing subordinates and dealing with colleagues.   This is not true in the private sector and new skills are required.

Both the former officer and the military member have operated from a tax-based budget system. The concept of profit-and-loss is often new to them and this too requires a change in thinking.

Rigidity is perhaps the biggest concern when considering this former police officer or military person. Often former public sector members have become ingrained within the rules and regulations under which they operate. After years of being comfortable in this mode, the transition to a private sector in which more sophisticated management skills are required is difficult. For some, it is impossible.

An extremely successful and innovative GM in a four-star property in Washington, D.C. swears by a method he developed which has proven very successful over the years. When the protection department manager position becomes available, he advertises for a recent graduate from a college or university who has majored in hotel management and desires to spend a career in lodging.

The GM believes that the ideal place for a new graduate to begin a successful career is as a manager in the protection department.

His reasoning is that the new employee will learn more about the entire property and its various departmental functions faster as a protection department manager than from any other prospective in the organization.

The new employee becomes involved in literally every department-- interfaces with literally every manager and most employees and encounters more problems and management decisions, than any of his colleagues who might be hired into another function.

Irrespective of the source from which the GM chooses his protection department manager, he should use the same care in that selection which he exhibits in hiring *any* manager for indeed the selected employee should be capable of becoming a vital link in the total property operation.

ORGANIZATION

As important as the criterion for selecting the protection manager is, the determination of the complexion of the organization itself is of equal importance. The most often posed question (aside from the "type" force to be chosen) is that of size. Also, to be considered are job requirements and the "look" of the force.

Size of force The size of the force (and the attendant cost)   if often the first question which arises in the mind of lodging management. This is unfortunate and suggests that the value added and return-on-investment aspects of the force are secondary to the cost of the force.

For example: consider a lodging facility which has no F&B operation and one is being considered. The initial thinking which goes into this decision is not the cost of the anticipated venture but rather the value-added and return-on-investment potential. (So should it be when considering a protection force.)

Therefore, when considering the size of a protection force, the manager should use the same management-science guidelines used in any organizational decision. He should develop this force with the three basic management considerations in mind:

Is this function required?

Is this function "doable?"

How can this function be made most operationally effective, cost efficient, and how can it ultimately favorably impact on the bottom line?

The "size" of the force, then, becomes a question answerable only after considering all aspects of the operation. The number of guards required normally depends on a careful analysis of the guard expectations regarding the five (or six) basic functions which you now know to be control, patrol, escort, inspection, emergency response, and training.

The protection manager needs to return again and carefully analyze each of the six functions in terms of the needs and requirements of his property.

> Will the control function be required and if so, how often, how widespread, and for what period of time?
>
> Will the patrol function be required (walking or by vehicle) and if so how often, how widespread, and for what scheduled or unscheduled activities?
>
> Will the escort function be required and if so how often, to what areas both on and off the property, and will vehicles be required or appropriate?
>
> Will the inspection function be required and if so, how often, and to what degree?
>
> Will the emergency response function be required and if so, to what extent?
>
> Will the training function be required and if so, to what extent?

Only after careful analysis of the factors may a determination be made of the size of the force required. If this seems difficult and beyond the normal experience of a new protection manager, he might ask himself if there is indeed much difference between this organizational management exercise and one which would be expected in, say, manning the newly conceived F&B function discussed above. Would not the F&B manager (like the protection manager) go through the same management process? He would be expected to do so in order to determine prior to deciding on the size of his F&B staff.

Here are more questions, the answers to which (because protection may be involved) will affect the protection force size decisions:

Will food service be available at all hours? In how many locations? Will it include room service? Will all locations be full service?

Will beverage service (with attendant lounge problems) be available at all hours? In how many locations? Will all locations be full service? How many patrols should be expected in each location? At what hours?

Will training be required of food servers? How many? How often? How about training for beverage servers? How much, how often, how many?

The comparisons above are obvious, as well as the point that there is no magical before-the-fact formula by which the size of a protection force may be determined.

Just as in the case of the F&B department and, for that matter, every department basic management analysis is required before determining this fact.

Protection officer position requirements   The characteristics--personal, professional, social--which surround the ideal guard are perhaps no different than those which any ideal employee should exhibit. Some considerations should be viewed, however, when considering employing protection officers. He, unlike probably any other employee...

...is often given more unrestricted, unmonitored and unsupervised access to more of the property's assets (particularly the guest) than any other single employee.

...is often the first property employee whom a guest (or visitor or vendor) encounters and from whom the first impression is gained.

...is usually the first person to interface with a guest or visitor or vendor when an untoward incident occurs.

Given these considerations (and visualizing both the value and the potential harm which could ensue) it is a prudent protection manager who gives special attention to the position requirements when selecting protection officers.

<u>Character</u>   There is no more important trait unequivocally required by a protection officer than that of honesty and reliability.

He must be, above all, absolutely above reproach in his personal character attributes. Depending on the particular tasks to which he is assigned, other character traits come, vitally, into play. He should be well disciplined and both able and adept when interfacing with other people and events in various types of situations. Some situations may be dangerous, some stressful, many difficult. His character should be such that he can adapt to these changing and challenging circumstances and represent the property well in all roles.

<u>Education</u>   A study was conducted of the private security industry, its employees, structure characteristics and salary considerations, in 1971. Although more than 25 years old (although updated in 1972) this study, *The Private Police Industry: Its nature and extent* (Santa Monica, CA: The Rand Corporation, 1971), Vol. 3, p.153 remains both current and seemingly accurate even today. The following quote dramatically portrays the "state-of-the-art" insofar as protection officers (then termed "private guards") are concerned:

> "The typical private guard is an aging white male who is poorly educated and poorly paid. Depending on where in the country he works and on his type of employer (contract guard firm, in-house firm, government), he has the following characteristics: His average age is between 40 and 55, he has had little education beyond the ninth grade; he has had a few

years of experience in private security; he earns a
marginal wage per hour and often works 48 to 56
hours per week to make ends meet. If employed part-
time, he works only 16 to 24 hours per week. Often
he receives few fringe benefits; at best, fringe benefits
may account to 10 percent of wages. Guards have
diverse backgrounds. Many are unskilled; some have
retired from a low-level Civil Service or military
career; younger part-timers are often students,
teachers, and military personnel on active duty.
Annual turnover rates range from less than 10 percent
in some in-house employment to 299 percent and
more in some contract firms. Few guards are
unionized."

From these examples, a protection manager can readily observe that
the type labor pool from which protection officers have, in the past,
been picked is not particularly encouraging. Even more alarming are
these portrayals when one remembers, as highlighted earlier, that
these employees hold THE KEYS TO THE VAULT.

A GM allows them (more accurately, *directs* them) to be the
protectors of the guest, the guardian of fixed assets, the respondent to
life-and-death situations, the lifeline between emergencies and
outside help. And yet, if you accept the above description, the GM
hires from "aging, poorly education, underpaid, applicants."

The "look" of the protection force: Several considerations and
options present themselves to management insofar as "the look" of
the force is concerned:

Uniforms and equipment

Communications

Arms

Gender

Uniforms and equipment   There is no hard and fast rule regarding how or whether to uniform and equip the protection force.

Possibilities range from no uniform whatsoever (ergo no uniformity) to a rigid police-like look complete with rank and insignia and the attendant equipment trappings. The decision, of course, should be made consistent with the ways this countermeasure is to be used and in what arena.

Most properties have opted for a middle-of-the road look--neither totally casual nor militarily rigid.

Typically, the protection officer in contemporary settings will be dressed, consistent with the season and weather and duty location, with a blazer, slacks, neckwear and with optional items including bad-weather gear, boots, and topcoat or a heavy jacket.

Equipment requirements will, of course, vary from property to property and from assignment to assignment, but the issue of a flashlight and communications equipment is virtually a given.

Communications   It is difficult to overemphasis the importance of management having the ability to communicate with protection officers on-duty and on-post and, in turn, providing them with the same ability.

The nature of emergencies is such that the ability to communicate and thereby respond quickly and effectively is paramount. Protection officers, obviously, cannot be at all places at all times. When emergencies arise, they must be dispatched quickly and efficiently.

Further, protection officers themselves often encounter emergencies (sometimes dangerous to themselves) and the need to call for assistance is great. Only an effective communication system can address these needs.

In a fixed-post assignment, telephones are normally adequate. However, when a protection officer is on patrol or on surveillance duty or elsewhere when telephones are inappropriate, quick and reliable communication must be available.

While in some uncommon cases one-way communications are all that is required, a pager system may be adequate. More often, however, two-way communications are not only desirable but necessary and such a system should be utilized.

Technology is changing virtually on a daily basis so the prudent protection department manager will carefully examine and weigh his options before this usually considerable investment is made.

Firearms   In Las Vegas, Nevada, in the late '70s when the movement of public corporations into the gaming industry increased, protection professionals from those corporations were confronted with what was, for many of them, a new challenge. *The management of virtually every casino in the city had equipped its protection officers with sidearms!*

Not only that, but when this was questioned by senior management from the incoming public corporations, the usual reaction was: "Of course we arm our guards! How else can we protect our cash?"

Fortunately, for the most part, this attitude--not only in Nevada but elsewhere--has changed considerably. In truth, there are only rare instances in which protection officers should (or need to be) armed. *When one considers that most sworn police officers spend their entire careers and retire without ever having to fire their weapons, it is difficult to justify arming private protection officers.*

There are, of course, throughout the entire spectrum of private security exceptions to this guideline. Private guards at a sensitive military-industrial complex, for instance, could be cited as an example.

Within the lodging industry, however, it is rare indeed that arms are a necessity. For every "excuse" to arm a protection officer, there are a multitude of reasons not to.

Liability is a major consideration. Perhaps even more significant is the real and inherent danger in increasing the exposure of guests and other employees to an already explosive life threatening situation by bringing arms into the conflict.

The best universal advice from virtually every expert in this field is when a circumstance seems so fraught with danger as to seem to require the introduction of firearms, then management should take one of two paths: either cancel/adjust the circumstances or, if this is impracticable, use only off-duty police officers as an armed component.

Many lodging chains further limit or prohibit other devices which can be considered as offensive weapons including mace and other chemical substances, night sticks, etc. Regardless of the decision made, it should not be the decision of the protection manager independently. Concurrence is necessary from either the Risk Management department, the legal department or both!

TYPE OF FORCE

When a determination has been made that indeed a protection force is appropriate on a property, the GM has at least three categories of protection officers from which to choose. These include contract personnel, proprietary officers and off-duty police officers. All have both advantages and disadvantages.

Contract Guard Services   These services are available in virtually all areas in which lodging properties exist. These services are offered by firms which specialize in the recruiting, hiring, training, and supervising of guards and subsequently contracting with entities such as hotels to supply that entity with these persons.

Commonly perceived advantages:

> Less expensive than either of the other two categories
>
> Less training time required
>
> Less administrative time required (HR files, etc.)
>
> Easily available replacements
>
> Less danger of disadvantageous relationships with staff
>
> Less property liability

Commonly perceived disadvantages:

> Less physical or intellectually qualified than other categories
>
> Present less of a professional image
>
> Less interested in loyalty to the property
>
> Higher turn over resulting in unstable protection force
>
> Likely to be disregarded because of "Rent-A-Cop" image

Proprietary Protection force   Many properties (and especially most protection department managers) prefer to develop their own in-house proprietary protection force. Properties, usually through their protection department manager, typically recruit through established classified means, interview, screen, hire and train just as they would any other property department employee.

Commonly perceived advantages:

> Better quality "handpicked" employees
>
> Better training potential
>
> Less turnover
>
> More chance of loyalty to property
>
> Higher potential for confidentiality and trustworthiness

Commonly perceived disadvantages:

> More potential for undesirable collusion with staff
>
> Likelihood of job "stagnation" or boredom
>
> High liability exposure
>
> More training required
>
> More supervision required
>
> More administrative support required

<u>Off Duty Police Officers</u>   In many, perhaps most, police jurisdictions, police officers commonly are available to "moonlight" and make themselves available for part-time employment. Serving as a protection officer is a common choice.

Commonly perceived advantages:

Exceptionally well trained

Provides on-site a sworn law enforcement capability

Can be employed with and is obviously trained in weapons

Presents a strong image.

Commonly perceived disadvantages:

Often extremely expensive

Presents an *unwanted* image to staff and guests

Potential for being called to other police duty without notice

Difficult to manage

Have an enforcement (reactive) mind-set rather than one of prevention (proactive)

This selection decision is not an easy one. The following guidelines, which, if consistent with the design and requirements of the force, should assist protection managers in force selection.

It is often advantageous to start such a force with an absolute skeleton force of proprietary guards and supplement them with contract guards as required. This approach offers several advantages.

More exact manning factors and needs can be realized after a trial period. If the initial estimate of staff requirements is in excess of what eventually develops, then the ability to reduce staff from within the contract personnel is far less complicated than adjusting staff numbers from a proprietary guard force.

Similarly, the required hours of coverage can be more easily adjusted if such coverage was over or underestimated initially. Specifically, if on a given shift, extended hours are found to be needed, such an adjustment using a contract force, is initially easier than having to adjust hours of proprietary employees.

Although contract guard firms often frown on this practice (some even contractually prohibit it) it may be to the advantage of the property to "field-test" a certain number of contract guards. If they, in fact, perform at a high quality level, they may be potential permanent hires when and if the proprietary guard portion of the force needs to be expanded. In such cases, care should be taken to acknowledge properly and reward the guard firm from whom the officer has been taken--perhaps by continuing or extending the contract.

When considering hiring off-duty police officers, such a decision should be a considered one. It should be made on an ad hoc basis and usually under special circumstances. There are several reasons for this position.

Often the temptation to hire off-duty police officers is steeped in frustration or anxiety. If a major event is planned, for instance, one in which crowd, traffic, or pedestrian control promises to be difficult. Subliminally, the GM may think that having an armed force on the property is to his advantage. These circumstances are fraught with potential liability but they also invite a careful management analysis. For instance:

> If the event is of such potential explosiveness that armed off-duty police are needed, is the potential profit indeed worth the exposure?

> If the event presents such challenges that police officers are needed, are there other temporary countermeasures which

241

would suffice such as higher access control, increased lighting, etc.?

Will the long range reputation of the property be adversely affected if off-duty police are required during events?

These questions and others must be made individually at each property by each affected manager. Because of the potential for disaster, however, they should be addressed long before the event occurs.

Whatever the decision, whether in-house proprietary, contract, off-duty police officers or some combination thereof, the goal and responsibility assigned to the protection manager is that of providing a guard force which will ultimately help in achieving the required level of guest protection--THAT OF REASONABLE CARE.

The selection, training, and supervision, then, of the selected force must meet that goal regardless of the type of guard utilized.

If the protection manager decides to staff (fully or partially) with contract guards, he must avoid the temptation to also contract the "responsibility" and decision making to that contract agency.

This must not happen.

Even if a contract agency is hired as the entire protection guard force even including supervisors and managers, the property retains the ultimate responsibility for guest protection and reasonable care. Such responsibility cannot be delegated; to attempt to do so only results in more complicated liability exposure and increases the likelihood that threats and exposures will develop about which senior management is unaware.

It follows then that *someone on staff* must be designated as responsible for this phase of guest protection and reasonable care.

That person must understand and be intimately familiar with the entire scope of the department. He and he alone must be held accountable for the conduct of the department--the decision, the aims, the thrust. Such accountability, as discussed in chapter one is essentially to ensure a proper protection level. This employee can delegate authority, but **must retain the responsibility and accountability.**

Beyond his responsibility and accountability, the person so designated (presumably the now-in-place protection manager) is faced with doing just that---managing.

Recall in an earlier chapter the clown model and the four M words which designated the tools with which the manager can "manipulate" his assigned management opportunity and achieve success. They are Money, Machinery, Methods, and Manpower. It is this first tool, this M for manpower tool, that here becomes significantly different from any of the other three.

> Manpower is almost invariably the most expensive of the tools

> Manpower is the most difficult of the tools to manipulate

> Manpower is the tool most often in need of "repair" or "adjustment"

> *Manpower is, however, the tool which can and should be far and away the most valuable, the most versatile, the one which can (if managed correctly) literally "do the job alone."*

In short, more time usually is spent, as well it should be, manipulating this tool than all others combined.

These considerations, of course, apply to whatever type security guard force the protection manager decides to develop. They are highlighted here, however, because it is during the utilization of contract guard force tools that the manager most often fails to manage properly.

The decision regarding which type of guard force to use is usually not an easy one. However, if the decision is made to utilize contract services, there are guidelines which can be extremely helpful as well as money and timesaving in the long run. The following is a list of considerations with which a manager should concern himself.

CONSIDERATIONS WHEN SELECTING A CONTRACT SECURITY FIRM

* License: Most states require commercial contract security firms to be licensed. Require a copy of the current certificate.

* Experience: Require a demonstrable record of experience, not only general security contract background but particularly in background in the lodging industry.

* Reputation: Require references with which you are comfortable.

* Employee Screening: Although you should perform pre-employment verification (including contract guards) require that the firm you are considering show evidence of performing this function also.

* Insurance: Determine your state's statutory insurance coverage requirement. Contact the security firms and require that a certificate of insurance be supplied. IMPORTANT: Get terms and conditions approval from your risk management or legal department.

* Training: Verify that the firm's entry-level as well as in-service training program is satisfactory and consistent with your requirements. HINT: Attend one of their training sessions.

* Post Orders: Post orders, ideally, are developed by you and published by the contract security firm.

* Reports: Inspect and approve all recurring and special reports the firm prepares. Add or modify appropriately.

* Supervision: If you are hiring supervision (which, in turn should be supervised by you) establish the specific conditions (e.g., on-site, off-site and schedule) of operation.

* Written proposal/contract: All aspects of the security guard/property agreements must be in written proposal and contract form. It is important to get terms and conditions approval from your risk management or legal department.

OTHER CONSIDERATIONS

Other services Devote ample negotiating time to allow investigation into and agreement on other or extraordinary services the firm offers or you desire.

Once a contract firm has been selected, the task of actually manning the protection department begins. Virtually every contract guard firm in its proposals, advertising, and practice will portray itself as a firm offering superior personnel and services. The protection manager should not allow himself to be lulled into accepting specifically what the firm has to offer just simply because *it is offered.*

Guard selection/assignment It is strange but all too true that protection managers often accept virtually, without question, the guards who are assigned to them. This is but another example of "passing off" the protection responsibility and should never occur. On the contrary, guards who are presented initially to the protection manager should be considered *applicants.*

They should be interviewed, tested, critiqued, and judged just as if they were applicants for any sensitive position. If they meet the protection manager's criterion, they may be brought onboard. If however (and this happens time and time again considering the limited labor pool from which they were chosen) they fail to meet the standards the protection manager has established, they should be returned to the contract firm and replacements demanded. This process should continue until the guards who are offered meet the manager's standards and requirements.

Guard training Normally, the lodging protection manager will desire that the protection officer he brings onboard from the contract security firm be trained. However, that statement begs the question: "Trained in what?"

The protection manager should refer back to his basics which were discussed earlier regarding the various functions he expects the guards to perform. It is very probable that regardless of the level and type training which the contract guard brings to the job, the protection manager will decide that his property's protection needs are such that significant additional training is required.

He cannot expect or even hope that the basic training the guard has received at his parent firm is anywhere near the level of, or specific to, what he wants the guards on his property to have. Thus additional training will be required.

Pre-assignment training, often required in the lodging industry and more often than not conducted prior to being assigned, include such subjects and concerns as:

Specific *lodging* protection duties: Since the guest is the prime asset and often the guest and the guard interface, it is vital that the guard must appreciate and be capable and willing to meet the challenge of guest protection.

Specific property rules with particular emphasis on those rules which the guard will be expected to enforce or react to.

Physical aspects of the property--including location, identity, character, function, and responsibility of each department.

Existing safety, security and firefighting procedures.

Location and proper operation of all fire and emergency equipment.

Emergency response expectations.

Areas or subjects of greatest concern (e.g., those areas of high risk or where the guest is most vulnerable.)

Locations and proper operation of emergency, electrical and HVAC control panels and switches, fuse boxes, steam valves, and hydrants.

Locations and proper operation of valves controlling water supply to the fire suppression system.

This list is not intended to be complete. Again, every property is unique and with that comes uniqueness in the protection requirements and methods. Each protection manager must develop his own guard training program to meet the needs of his property.

Once that list is complete (and it requires constant review and updating) the protection manager has the option of several training approaches or a combination thereof. (Refer to chapter nine.)

Initial training upon employment

Classroom (both initial and in-service)

Correspondence or home study

On-the-job

Written instructions, often among the most effective methods of training/control.

Guard attitude/demeanor/appearance It is not uncommon to receive from a contract guard service a prospective guard whose general demeanor does not meet the expectations of the client protection manager. Often that applicant falls below the standards expected. Sometimes he may be of an ilk more military or enforcement-like than the manager desires.

Regardless of what shortcomings prospective guards arrive with, the protection manager often finds it appropriate to mold them into the general demeanor he desires.

Guidelines for which protection managers often strive in general appearance and deportment are usually aimed toward the model guard who:

Gives a favorable first impression

Invites respect

Transmits an aura of confidence, capability, and easy authority

Enhances morale

Communicates easily and effectively

Exhibits exemplary conduct at all times.

POINTS TO PONDER

PROTECTION OFFICERS

◆   Discuss reasons why the term "protection officers" may be preferable to "security officer."

◆   Identify the five basic functions which a protection officer is generally expected to perform.

◆   Discuss a scenario which illustrates each of these functions.

◆   Discuss how the sixth function, that of training, could appreciably add to a property protection profile.

◆   Discuss the position that it is often difficult for a former police officer to become an effective protection manager.

◆   Discuss generally how the decision regarding "force size" may be reached.

◆   Discuss the importance of communications capability within a protection department.

◆   Discuss the arguments which may go into the decision of providing weapons to a protection department.

◆   Identify the three most common types of protection force.

◆   Discuss at least two perceived advantages and disadvantages of each of the three.

CHAPTER FOURTEEN

GUESTROOM PROTECTION

The setting and the challenge.

With the possible exception of pre-employment verification, guestroom protection is perhaps the most significant countermeasure which management should develop and maintain.

Consider the facts. It is in the guestroom that the guest spends the majority of his time, and the majority of that time is sleeping, which obviously renders him more vulnerable than during waking hours. Furthermore, it is normally the case that during these nighttime hours the staff (and the attendant protection) is at its lowest level. It follows, then, that guestroom protection must be well planned, comprehensive in its application and managed/monitored effectively.

The guestroom, ideally, is designed and maintained to give the impression of and also actually provide comfort, convenience, restfulness and security. These are not unlike the considerations a person strives for in his own home. Innkeepers, as hosts, typically attempt to duplicate that secure feeling of being in one's own home, as well as provide the amenities which they believe the guest has in his home. Furniture, sleeping accommodations, bathroom facilities, well-lighted spaces are but a few of the attempts to duplicate the guest's own residence--all in the interest of guest satisfaction.

What Innkeepers must realize is that personal safety and security in the home have been developed over the lifetime of the owner's residence. They have been developed and maintained and updated as the resident/owner sees fit, depending on the assets he wishes to protect--usually his family and his possessions. He's been aware of and has provided for the threats against which he sees those assets exposed. He is familiar with his neighborhood, the history of crime and the protection afforded by local police, by neighbors, and by his own protection program.

In a lodging setting, however, the guest, unless he is informed, cannot be expected to understand and appreciate the threats that exist which are peculiar to that city, that neighborhood or to that property.

Furthermore, although he has a certain obligation to assist in his own protection, he cannot be expected to provide his own "protection package." On the contrary, he comes with a variety of traveling and self-protection experience which may range from virtually none to extensive, and it should be assumed that he, the traveler, has the expectation of being protected.

And he has the right to such an expectation!

IDENTIFICATION OF THREATS

The threats which a guest faces in his guestroom are seemingly unlimited. Certainly any threat common to the lodging industry and shown in the Protection Management Matrix may exist in the guestroom.

Obviously the nature of each threat, the significance of it and the protection considerations against it will vary from property to property (ergo the uniqueness of the property protection plan discussed throughout this text.) There are, however, some protection considerations which are virtually universal and which should be incorporated into any guestroom protection countermeasures.

Guestroom protection begins at the front desk.

Keys, irrespective of the keying system utilized, ideally, should not advertise the name of the property.

NOTE: While guestroom protection, as a countermeasure, stands alone, it is so vital that several complimentary countermeasures are also addressed in this chapter.

More and more properties are employing a method by which even the guestroom door number is not shown. Rather, that identification is either encoded on the guestroom key and the guest provided with the decoding instructions or other methods to inform the guest of the room number.

Confidentiality of the guestroom location is vital. No audible announcement of the guest's room number should be made at the front desk or at any location. When providing the key to the guest, he should be informed of the room number by the use of a card or key holder or some other nonverbal means. Obviously, when the bell staff is used, the room number again should never be verbalized but rather the bellperson should be informed of the room location in the same confidential manner by which the guest was notified.

When receiving inquiries regarding a guest, whether by phone or in person, the confidentiality must again be maintained. A guest's right to privacy is a vital and longstanding tenant of lodging and should never be violated.

When a request is made for a room key by a person claiming to be an occupant of that room, positive identification must be made of that person prior to issuing a key. Standard identification methods should be established and used as appropriate. Some examples are:

*   Showing positive picture identification and comparing the name to that on the folio. (Note: It is obvious that if a single room was rented to a "Mrs. Smith" then the desk clerk should question the validity and authorization of a "Mr. Smith" receiving a duplicate key.)

* When the requesting person claims to have forgotten his identification or left it in his room, verification should be required by some other means. Such means include: requiring him to indicate the zip code shown on the folio or identifying the credit card used during check in. Always check the folio, and when an accompanying guest is registered in the same room, a phone call to verify identity and authorization might be in order.

* In addition, when there is any doubt, have the person escorted to the room so that proper identification can be authenticated.

* When a second or subsequent key is issued, a notation of that fact should, of course, be placed in the folio.

LOCKS AND PORTALS -- THE NEXT LINE OF PROTECTION

Locks   The locking system utilized at the guestroom door is a major consideration in this countermeasure we have called guestroom protection. Basically systems available to the Innkeeper fall into one of four general categories:

(1) Key in knob   As the name implies, this is a system in which the key channel is actually within and a part of the door knob itself. It is activated by inserting the key directly into the knob   and the channel. This is probably the least effective of all systems, is considered generally insecure and in fact is prohibited in some states as a hotel/motel guestroom locking system.

(2) Standard mortise locks   The word "mortise" means, literally, "a hole, groove or slot into or through which some other part of an arrangement of parts fits or

passes." This system usually consists of a face plate, with the doorknob and an unconnected separate key channel on the exterior side of the door and a deadbolt arrangement on the interior side of the door.

(3)   <u>Mortise locks with programmable cylinders and/or removable cores</u>   These allow for quick key combination changes.

(4)   <u>Electronic lock systems</u>   These allow for a unique selection of keying combinations whenever a new guest is assigned to that room, whenever a compromise or key loss is suspected and whenever management determines that such action is warranted.

Obviously new and more sophisticated systems are reaching the market on a continuing basis and the choice for the Innkeeper is a difficult one. If there is a single rule-of-thumb to follow, it is that whatever system is chosen, it offers higher protection if the locking combination can be changed on a random or programmed basis whenever required.

<u>The main guestroom door</u> Door and frame construction as well as attendant locking hardware should be of such quality and workmanship as to minimize the ease by which an intruder can bypass them by force.

Obviously, the hinges should be located to preclude the pins being pulled from the exterior. Glass, either in the door (very rare and not recommended) or in a panel near the door, should be of such strength and of such configurations as to minimize the possibility of an intruder breaking it and reaching into the room and accessing the locking system

The lock bolt should be configured to minimize forceful entry and of such strength as to minimize being cut. Self closing automatic locking devices should be standard.

Connecting doors Connecting room doors are those doors which are placed between guestrooms to allow for access from one guestroom to another or to enlarge the rented space from one-room to two-or-more-room capacity. Historically, these doors often have been of lesser construction than the main guestroom door. In fact, the threat which is posed to the guest by inappropriate connecting room door design, maintenance or construction warrants special attention.

Single connection door arrangements are strongly discouraged. Instead, there should be two separate doors, each void of all hardware (save perhaps a blank plate) on the inside. In effect, then, there are two doors facing one another, neither with locking hardware and with space between them. On the guestroom side of each door, however, there should be provision for the guest himself to provide added self-protection (e.g., dead bolts with a minimum throw of one inch.) Only guests occupying both rooms simultaneously and in concert with one another or hotel/motel staff should have the ability to access both rooms.

Additional doors Care should be given to securing any additional access doors into the guestroom. Sliding glass doors, patio doors, etc. should be equipped with locking devices and secondary devices should be considered (e.g., movement restricting bars called "charlie bars," chains or pin protective devices.)

DOOR DEVICES

View ports (commonly but incorrectly often referred to as peepholes) should be installed in the guestroom door. The exception to this guideline would be in the case of those door/room configurations in which adjacent glass paneling allows observation of anyone immediately outside the guestroom door. A minimum 200-degree viewing angle is considered acceptable.   A second view port for disabled persons is recommended and is in fact required in rooms complying with the Americans with Disabilities standards.

Secondary and additional protective equipment is appropriate on the main guestroom door, depending on the locking system utilized. Many door locking systems have a double locking dead bolt and single action panic release features installed within the system. Consideration should be given to adding safety chains or dead bolts or both.

Postings and Notices   Innkeepers often fall into the habit of assuming that guests are all sophisticated, seasoned travelers. This simply is not the case (many are first time travelers--all guests were at one time-- others are simply inattentive, unaware and all too trusting.)   Innkeepers owe to all guests not only installed and managed protection but also the opportunity and means of protecting themselves. Guestroom postings and other written notices in English and any other appropriate languages are one method of accomplishing this requirement. Postings should be well designed, well maintained, easily accessible, easily read and easily understood.

Innkeepers law   Many states require the Innkeepers laws of that state to be posted prominently within the guestroom. The limits of liability insofar as the loss of personal belongings are normally shown and are posted so that the guest understands those limits. Also, normally noted on these postings are the considerations of safe deposit and property safekeeping facilities available at the property. All too often, however it is the Innkeeper himself who has not kept his knowledge current. He is well advised to do so.

Door-locking considerations   Announcements concerning what actions the guest ought to take in order to secure that door to the fullest extent possible should be posted on or near the back of the guestroom door. Use of the safety chain, if applicable, should be explained as should the use, if appropriate, of the dead bolt. All double locking procedures should likewise be explained. Use of the view port and methods of securing any connecting or sliding/patio doors should also be addressed.

Safety postings   Personal injuries due to accidents occur more often in the bathroom than any other portion of the guestroom. Postings, therefore, regarding tub safety, use of any grab bars, slip-and-fall deterrent bath mats, etc. should be considered. If particular use of electrical equipment in the bathroom is desired, warnings regarding their use should be posted.

Smoking considerations   Many properties offer nonsmoking rooms. If a room has been so designated, this fact should be posted on the exterior of the guestroom as well as prominently displayed within the room itself. In rooms in which smoking is permitted, local fire codes should be constantly reviewed and appropriate fire prevention procedures and advice posted accordingly.

The telephone   The guestroom telephone is more than a convenience. It can be, literally, a lifesaving guest protection device. Consider posting prominently and distinctly on the phone faceplate a notation of the number to be called to summon help. Consider a notation, for instance, printed in red, bold print, announcing that assistance may be summoned by dialing "111" or some other assigned number.

Of even greater concern, obviously, is the system devised to both answer immediately and prioritize any emergency calls.   Several methods are possible to accomplish this immediate handling of any emergency call.

      *   The emergency number can be channeled, like all operator calls, into a central switchboard. If this is the system chosen, care should be taken that when the emergency number is dialed, it has an extremely distinct ring--much louder perhaps or with a distinct tone.

    *   The use of a warning light which is activated along with the distinct ring adds greater assurance that the operator will note the call immediately and cease all other duties to respond to it.

    *   The emergency line might also be channeled into a continually manned security office, dispatch point or control center. Again, the ringing apparatus and arrangement must be such that the ringing annunciation is clear, distinct and unique and is inevitably responded to immediately. Consideration should be given to installing a system so that the room number is displayed when a call is received. Automatic taping of the ensuing conversation is a plus.

    *   Some hotel chains/properties have adopted a procedure whereby the guest is advised to dial an outside number such as 911 to request emergency assistance. Great care and planning are essential before such a procedure is established.

Whatever method of immediate response is adopted, the recipient of the call, whether a front desk clerk, a switchboard operator or a security officer, <u>must be trained and scripted in quick and accurate response</u>.

Many municipalities using the nearly universal 911 system have developed scripting which is quick and concise and makes misinterpretation or extraneous conversation a minimal concern. Immediate response announcement such as "This is the emergency operator, Mr. (Guest's name), what is the nature of your emergency?" go far to calm an understandably excited caller. This professional and informed response goes far to reduce conversation to the minimum thus allowing quick and appropriate action.

<u>The Guestroom Service Directory</u>   Many properties place within the guestroom a booklet announcing both in-house amenities and nearby products, services and shops in which the guest might have an interest. This booklet is an ideal place to prominently display protection information. Some subjects which might appear as appropriate include discussions and/or directions concerning:

* The emergency phone number and what response can be expected when calling it.

* All aspects of security within the room. Use of the safety chain, use of the dead bolt, use of any double locking devices available should be mentioned. While this should also be posted on the interior side of the guestroom door, repeating it in the Guest Service Directory is an added measure of guest protection.

* Safety considerations such as use of grab bars, auto-slip mats, etc.

* Use of the view port

* Care in allowing visitors access to the room.

* Use of the safe deposit system.

* Fire (or other emergency) alarm system. Describe how the alarms sound and what action the guest is expected to take.

* Safe smoking guidance.

* Lawful (and unlawful) use of the courtesy bar.

These listings and notifications should be unique to the property as the property and its protection are unique. Consideration should be given to listing each and every possible threat and protection circumstance with which the guest may come into contact.

The lodging industry is long past the time when it was felt that education of guests about threats and dangers and protection methods were contrary to the "host image." On the contrary, such announcements and notifications are now considered absolutely essential by most professional hoteliers.

<u>In-room television announcements</u>   Several well-recognized lodging chains, in conjunction with the American Hotel & Motel Association and the Advertising Council, have developed in-room television announcements concerning protection. This is a useful and effective guest protection tool. It obviously may be produced in any number of formats but the most effective presentations seem to be those which are friendly (often a female presenter and narrator) effectively non-threatening and certainly designed to inform rather than to alarm. This technique is particularly valuable and useful with regard to the threat of fire and the activation of warning alarms and alert systems.

There is probably no more anxiety-provoking circumstance to the guest than to hear an alarm and not know what it means! Is there a fire? Is there an earthquake or natural disaster? Do I evacuate? Do I stay in my room?

Usually the first impulse is to open a door to the hall, look out and see what there is to see, and then call the front desk or operator. A little replanning can go a long way in preventing these circumstances.

<u>Bell staff announcements</u>   The bell staff should be scripted and instructed in all protection aspects of the guestroom. They should direct the guests to the TV announcement, if there is one, even turning the TV on and to the particular announcing channel so that the guest gets an early opportunity to view and hear it.

The bellperson should also call to the guest's attention the guestroom service directory and highlight the fact that there is a section regarding protection.

Finally, the bellperson should mention the entire range of protection devices, techniques and announcements present in the room. He should discuss all subjects ranging from the use of the door devices, safe deposit system to advice about safety and fire protection.

Of particular importance is having the bell staff explain the alarm system. They should describe what warnings are possible, what they mean, how they sound, and what the guest's response should be.

<u>Housekeeping inspections</u>   A program of   room attendant inspections of protection-related guestroom items should be established.   If a room attendant checklist is in use, the guest protection items which should be subject to inspection should be contained thereon.   If no such checklist system is in use, the guest protection items to be inspected should simply be added to whatever initial and in-service training program exists. The list of inspection items should include at a minimum:

Presence and condition of postings.

Presence and condition of door protection devices (safety chains, dead bolts, double locking device(s), single action panic release(s), door closures, and view ports.)

NOTE: It may be difficult to believe, but there are cases in which the view port   has been installed, either by accident or by design, <u>backwards!</u>

Presence and condition of bathroom and other safety devices.

Presence and condition of the guestroom service directory.

POINTS TO PONDER

GUESTROOM PROTECTION

◆   Discuss three reasons supporting the position that guestroom protection is a uniquely significant countermeasure.

◆   Determine what threats, if any, are not present in the guestroom.

◆   Explain why property names should not appear on guestroom keys.

◆   Give three examples of improper guestroom protection techniques sometimes observed at the front desk.

◆   Give a simple explanation of a mortise lock.

◆   Discuss what you consider to be the main advantage of an electronic locking system.

◆   Discuss what you consider to be the main disadvantage of an electronic locking system.

◆   Discuss basic protection considerations surrounding connecting guestroom doors.

◆   Describe the legal rationale for Innkeeper's Laws and the posting thereof in guestrooms.

CHAPTER FIFTEEN

EMERGENCY RESPONSE

A illustrative story is in order while introducing the subject of emergency response.

Attendees at a Fall hotel risk management symposium were lodged in a high-rise hotel located in a northern city. At approximately 4:30 a.m., an audible alarm sounded and a recorded voice directed all guests to evacuate.

Most were dressed in night clothing--few, if any, were prepared for cold and wet weather. Although there was the expected confusion and anxiety, there seemed to be no panic. Most guests, following specific instructions, evacuated the property by walking down the designated fire stairwell and exiting onto a main street. They found themselves on a city thoroughfare (fortunately void of traffic at this early hour), and with no further instructions from the hotel, they crossed the street and watched from the other side.

They observed the arrival of the municipal fire emergency crew and watched as they set up operations and entered the hotel. And they waited, and waited, and waited...

At approximately 5:00 a.m., they noticed activity in the hotel street-level breakfast buffet area--a large, well lit and well appointed room. They watched as a uniformed restaurant employee proceeded to set up for an apparently scheduled 6:00 a.m. continental breakfast. As they watched (and shivered) the F&B employee carefully and professionally, set up croissants, Danish, other expected menu items-- including vat after vat of hot coffee!!!

It is probable that the suffering guests' perception that the employee was both smirking slightly, and ignoring them consciously, was only an illusion. What was *factual*, however, was that great expense had gone into an effective early warning system which worked as planned. Yet apparently, little no thought or planning had gone into follow-on action (e.g., taking hot coffee out to comfort the guests.)

The attendees had received, during their stay, superlative conference-related service. Unfortunately, however, the amenities, and professionalism and superior service provided by the property were later forgotten; replaced by the ill feelings born of poor judgment and lack of planning.

It is appropriate to review the example above from the perspective of what should occur on any property during early morning hours when an alarm annunciates. Again, consider the events described above and the following questions.

*   What actions *ought* to be taken at 4:30 a.m. when a fire alarm annunciates?

*   Who should investigate? How will that person be notified and how will he report his findings?

*   Should the Fire Department *always* be called, if so *when-- before the local investigation is conducted, for instance* and by whom?

*   Who should decide if evacuation is required? And, if so:

    *   How will guests be notified?

    *   *Which* guests (which floors) will be notified?

* Are disabled guests registered on the property (if so, can the front desk locate them and provide assistance or special accommodations?)

* Is assistance and direction appropriate during the evacuation (if so, who will accomplish such action?)

* Is assistance and direction appropriate after the guests evacuate (if so, who will accomplish this?)

* Is there a "holding zone" (if so, who is in charge of it and what are that person's duties?)

* Who will direct the guests' return following the emergency?

And the questions may go on and go on and go on...

What of the answers...?

The high-rise evacuation scenario cited above is by no means unique. Consider another.

In the mid-90's a hotel risk management consultant was contracted to lecture to a group of GMs of a national franchise hotel chain. The subject was emergency response.

Each GM was requested to answer in writing the following question: "What *initial action* do you expect from your MOD if, during early morning hours, the front desk receives a call from a guest, complaining of `Smelling smoke.'"

Five very different answers were received from the twenty-one attendees.

"I expect him to call the fire department." (6 responses)

"I expect him to go to that floor and investigate (or have someone do so.") (5 answers)

"I expect him to call me." (4 answers!!!!)

"I leave it up to him." (3 answers)

"I don't know." (3 answers)

Some questions and analysis of the responses are in order.

Regarding group one's comments, fire departments differ in their policies on being called *as the first action* when smoke is reported. Perhaps, in each of the six responses, the property had indeed, coordinated with the fire service and that agency *had* directed that this action was appropriate. On the other hand, one wonders, in the absence of such pre-incident planning, how the fire department would react.

In the second group of responses, ("go to the floor and investigate") it appears likely, that emergency response planning had been on the agenda of those properties. (Or perhaps the responding GM *thought* that would be the best answer.)

The responses of the final three groups are particularly interesting.

*   "I expect him to call me." (an astounding near 25% of respondents)

What will he, the GM, do when he gets the call? Direct the MOD to call the fire department? Direct the MOD to investigate? Put him on hold while he, the GM, gets dressed and comes to take charge himself?

*   "I leave that up to him." (3 respondents)

This indicates, either an extremely high level of confidence in the MOD or (more likely) that this property has failed to address emergency response techniques.

*   Those who said, "I don't know" are perhaps the most interesting group of all. (3 respondents)

One wonders if they were simply honest (and went back to their properties and corrected the void) or indeed had gotten into the wrong line of work.

EMERGENCY RESPONSE PROCEDURES

Emergency response procedures, when viewed as one of the eight guest protection countermeasures, is unique in that it alone is *reactive* in nature.

We establish access control *proactively* to deter unauthorized access.

We develop key control *proactively* to strengthen protection.

We install lighting *proactively* to minimize unauthorized intrusion.

Indeed, with the exception of the countermeasure of emergency response, *all* countermeasures are designed *in anticipation* of a threat--emergency reaction, alone, as it's name implies, is designed to *respond* to threats.

The term "emergency response," is meant to incorporate several related terms, including Emergency Management, Disaster Control and Disaster Management. The publicity surrounding emergencies (particularly severe weather--witness the media coverage of disastrous hurricanes) has spawned many of these titles. Our term "emergency response" is meant to incorporate all of them.

The term "Emergency" crosses the boundaries of earlier identified threats. Within the lodging industry, emergencies generally fall into one of six categories:

*   Severe weather (including earthquakes)
*   Medical
*   Criminal
*   Fire
*   Public demonstrations/civil disturbances.
*   Significant accidents (e.g., chemical spills or transportation incidents)

NOTE: This chapter on emergency response is less a *how-to* chapter than *a what ought to be planned for* chapter. The reasons are obvious. Even a cursory examination of the six categories of emergencies above indicates that the sheer volume of possible emergency situations makes a "how-to" approach impractical.

Of even more significance, however is the fact that for every one of the multitude of possible emergency situations, there is also a of multitude of possible responses.

There are simply too many possible variables to engage in a *how-to* exercise. Proper guest protection and reasonable care does not normally require planning for all of them. Rather, it is usually sufficient for the property (through the protection management committee) to plan for an emergency response program aimed at that specific property. Again, the *planning* is appropriate for the protection management committee--the *training* focus which is obviously the necessary follow-on, is discussed in chapter nine.

Preparation for developing emergency response is generally begun as an agenda item of the protection management committee.

Both hotel management and the protection management committee are well advised to avail themselves of a document entitled: "Disaster

Planning Guide for Business and Industry," published by the Federal Emergency Management Agency (FEMA.) That guide, a portion of which has been utilized in this chapter, provides further guidelines in the planning and conduct of emergency response.

The initial responsibility of the protection management committee is the determination of the specific emergencies their property faces. Next they should consider the form and content of their response. They should then consider what means and resources are available (both from within the property and from exterior sources) to deliver such response.

NOTE: Arguably, no more difficult decision faces a MOD than that of *property evacuation*. Such questions as *when* to evacuate, *how* to evacuate and *who* to evacuate potentially face every MOD every day of the year. Therefore, evacuation considerations and answers should be a top priority when accomplishing emergency response planning.

Finally, and obviously only after the welfare of people has been addressed, the subjects regarding the return of the property to normal status should be considered.

The following is offered as a planning guide in developing the countermeasure of emergency response. The questions which follow each category constitute only a sample listing of the questions which the committee should address.

Weather Severe weather can be broken into five general categories: wind storms (hurricanes, tornados, typhoons); snow conditions (including ice and hail); flooding and a category in and of itself, severe temperatures (either extreme heat or extreme cold, not necessarily connected with any of the other weather conditions) and earthquakes.

While addressing this particular emergency, the protection management committee should use available resources and determine which of the various types of weather is common to their property and determine the appropriate action. The deliberations of the committee should include, generally, such as subjects as:

* How are warnings of each weather emergencies normally received at the property?

* What planning (e.g., stockpiling of supplies) is appropriate?

* What service or product or specific care is appropriate?

* How are such services or products to be delivered and by whom?

* If specific instructions are necessary, how are such instructions to be given?

* Who will be responsible for accomplishing various tasks at off hours when staffing is at its lowest level?

Medical Properties face the threat of medical emergencies at all hours, in and around all departments. Medical emergencies threaten guests, employees, vendors and visitors alike. Any medical situation may become a Medical Emergency--only the intensity of the situation will determine this. Such situations range from accidents and injuries (slips-and-falls, burns, cuts, blows from falling objects,) to illnesses (from the common to the bizarre,) to isolated occurrences (sudden childbirth or the death of an elderly guest from natural causes.)

When addressing the emergency, the protection management committee should consider, for example, the following:

* What level of emergency medical treatment is the property able and willing to supply?

* If *any* level is determined appropriate, who should deliver such treatment?

* How and by whom should staff be trained?

* What medical supplies are necessary and where should they be stored?

* When calling upon *outside* medical resources, how are they to be contacted and by whom?

Criminal   The list of criminal emergencies on a property is only limited by the number and identity of crimes listed in the penal codes of the particular state involved. Such listings may run alphabetically from Arson and Bomb Threats through Theft and Vandalism. With the possible exception of *bank robbery*, virtually every crime listed in the typical criminal codes *can, has* and *will* occur on lodging properties. The list of possible crimes is too long to enumerate and anticipate. A more realistic approach is one in which crimes are divided into two categories: property crimes and crimes against persons.

Property Crimes The most common lodging property crimes with which the lodging manager need be concerned are theft, burglary (particularly room burglary) and vandalism. While these criminal acts are burdensome, time-consuming and often expensive, they are of less concern when compared to crimes against persons.

Crimes against Persons Crimes against persons can be, and often are, the most devastating and traumatic experience with which a lodging manager has to deal in his professional career. Along with the threat of fire, the threat of a crime against one of his guests (or employees) looms constantly and threateningly. Instances of homicide, sexual assault, armed robbery, assault and battery, are the most common crimes against persons. Such crimes have figuratively torn properties apart, devastated lives and careers, and caused

273

physical, mental and emotional scars which sometimes are never erased.

*There is literally no crime against persons which can be ignored--all must be expected on every property. And, if the combination of the selected **proactive** countermeasures do not deter such events, effective **reaction** should be in readiness.*

When addressing the crime emergency, the protection management committee might consider such subjects as:

* What personal attention is appropriate for guests who have suffered a criminal loss (either the loss of property or a loss resulting from a crime against person?)

* What factors are to be considered when deciding whether to call the local police authorities?

* What factors are to be considered when deciding if and when to notify the insurance carrier?

* What actions and limitations are expected of staff following the discovery of a criminal act?

* What chain-of-command notifications are appropriate?

* What immediate actions are appropriate if an employee is suspected of being responsible for a criminal act?

Fire Recall that earlier in the text, "Fire" was identified as probably the single most significant threat which the lodging industry faces. Given its potential for disastrous and life-threatening magnitude, the

274

subject of fire should be given the highest priority in terms of both prevention and response.

Arguably, in facing this threat, the lodging industry has progressed well. Aided and directed by governmental codes, the lodging industry has made great strides in the establishment and maintenance of effective preventive measures. Fire-resistant materials, annunciation capabilities and suppression techniques and methods are being addressed. In contrast to these technological advances, however, has been the lagging of the *people-response factor of this equation.*

Simply stated, the establishment of, and training in, emergency response techniques has not received the universal attention warranted. There should be no higher priority for the protection management committee than that of addressing the threat of fire.

To insure the maximum possible protection, emergency response to the fire threat should be property-specific. Depending upon the capabilities and sophistication of the fire system on the property (i.e., detection, annunciation and suppression) the property should plan a response program accordingly.

According to FEMA, "The biggest single need (when encountering the fire threat) usually is not personnel and equipment. Most often it is the ability to respond quickly and to confine the fire to manageable limits before it reaches the disaster stage. This calls for a pre-fire plan of action for mutual aid response by existing local fire organizations."

This statement seems to set the stage for planning by the protection management committee. It should address such questions as:

> *   How often does the local fire authority inspect and what is the record of quick and effective response to those inspections?

*   What is the status of the fire detection system?

*   What is the status of the fire annunciation system?

*   What is the status of the fire suppression system?

*   Who inspects and maintains these systems?

*   Who is responsible for internal fire inspections in each department and on a continuing basis?

*   What staff training is appropriate for all levels of employees?

*   Is rapid and effective response available *and assured* at all times--particularly when staffing is at its lowest level?

Public demonstrations/civil disturbances Demonstrations, whether prompted by political action, labor unrest or any of a host of other motivations, should be considered as circumstances against which emergency response is appropriate.

Some demonstrations develop slowly, allowing the property to contact appropriate governmental assistance. Others may flare up with little advance warning (although there are often earlier indications of a buildup of tensions and pressures.)

The protection management committee should address such questions as:

*   What public demonstration/civil disturbance conditions should trigger a call to law enforcement authorities?

* What access control changes should be considered when a demonstration occurs?

* Is guest notification appropriate and, if so, in what form?

* What direct contact, if any, should be attempted between the staff and the demonstrators?

Accidents Major accidents which threaten the property and the lives of guests or employees are often (although not inevitably) transportation related. Virtually every lodging facility has the potential of being affected by a major accident involving air, highway, railroad or shipping services. Chemical spills on a nearby highway, an explosion or crash of an aircraft, a train derailment are but a few of the possibilities with which the property should be concerned. In planning for such emergencies, the protection management committee should follow the same approach described above for *any* emergency, i.e., determination of which major accident emergency is possible for the property; what exterior resources can and should be called for; and what immediate response should the staff affect.

After all planning for the response to the emergency--protection of life being always the first consideration--then the final step is appropriate. The protection management committee should concern itself with the subject of returning the property to normal operation.

POINTS TO PONDER

EMERGENCY RESPONSE

◆   Discuss the single most pronounced difference between the countermeasure of emergency response and all the other seven.

◆   Identify the six categories of emergencies which generally threaten the lodging industry.

◆   Give at least two examples of each.

◆   Identify the two basic types of criminal emergencies which threaten the typical property.

◆   Give at least two examples of each.

◆   Defend the position that all employees in all departments require emergency response training.

INDEX

INDEX

INDEX

INDEX

INDEX

INDEX

NOTES
Chapter 1: Connie Francis - the Terrible Beginning

NOTES
Chapter 2: Hotel Protection Management Theory

NOTES
Chapter 3: The Laws Affecting the Lodging Industry

NOTES
Chapter 4: Protection Management Matrix

NOTES
Chapter 5: Countermeasures

NOTES
Chapter 6: The Protection Management Survey

NOTES
Chapter 7: The Wagon Wheel and the Protection Management Committee

NOTES
Chapter 8:Pre-Employment Verification

NOTES
Chapter 9: Guest Protection Training

NOTES
Chapter 10: Access control

NOTES
Chapter 11: Lighting

NOTES
Chapter 12: Key Control

NOTES
Chapter 13: Protection Officers

NOTES
Chapter 14: Guestroom Protection

NOTES
Chapter 15: Emergency response